: "To-night the German astronomers ... the sky ... the moon will eclipse the planet ...
... look ...

German astronomers ... red spot ... Jupiter ... the eclipse will help ... learn ...
red spot ... are interested only in the red
... But our brave ... fears ... the red spot ...
... this folly ..."

An Ordinary Newsca...

This is perhaps the most ig... state we

heard yet ... We are not a ... people ...
... having been ... smacked ... into war, ...
... betrayed ...

it that ... our whole ... future ... peace ...
of that ... So ... will the ... it, ...
... credits, ... to humanity
in the course of our 43 war ... can ... sweeten it

... course of ...
Oc... ... Jupiter
... force.

January 13, '44
XI

IN THIS
WILD
WATER

IN THIS WILD WATER

The Suppressed Poems
of
ROBINSON JEFFERS

by

James Shebl

Ward Ritchie Press • Pasadena, California

8/1977
Am. Lit.

FOR PATRICIA

IN APPRECIATION

Gratefully, I acknowledge permission to publish material from the collection at The Humanities Research Center of the University of Texas in Austin. I should like to thank William Holman, director of the center, for the special efforts he and his staff provided.

I am indebted to Mr. and Mrs. Donnan Jeffers for permission to publish the manuscripts and for conscientious and gentle remarks.

I owe special appreciation to my editors, Louis Leiter, Charles Clerc, Diane Borden, and James Riddles, for whose criticisms and kindnesses I shall be ever grateful. I am deeply grateful to Arlen Hansen, whose very talented direction and generous friendship bolstered my *efforts* on more occasions than memory can provide.

CONTENTS

He considered the double-bladed Axe:
            "In Crete it was a
god, and they named the labyrinth for it. That's
            long
before the Greeks came; the lofty Greeks
            were still bush-
men. It was a symbol of generation: the
            two lobes and the
stiff helve: so was the Cross before they
            christened it. But
this one can clip heads too. Grimly,
            grimly. A blade for
the flesh, a blade for the spirit: and
            truth from lies."

PREFACE

The logic behind this book is quite straightforward. Through various and interesting social circumstances, I discovered that a number of unpublished Jeffers manuscripts, mostly holographs, had been purchased en masse from Donnan Jeffers, son of the late poet, who yet resides in Tor House in Carmel. The purchaser was an agent for the Humanities Research Center at the University of Texas at Austin.

My initial research brought to light the existence of two tables of contents to *The Double Axe and Other Poems,* along with the manuscripts of the poems published in that book and those of ten poems not published. My reading of the extensive correspondence between Robin and Una Jeffers in Carmel and Bennett Cerf, the president of Random House, and Saxe Commins, Jeffers' editor, pointed up the rationale for the two tables of contents: the one containing ten poems fewer than the other proved to be that of the 1948 published edition. It became clear that for one reason or another, poems from the manuscript originally submitted had been expunged.

A close reading of Jeffers' unprinted poems revealed, to a greater extent than previous critics had understood, the poet's philosophy of inhumanism, the philosophy that was so manifest in *The Double Axe.* Because this volume appeared at the time Jeffers' standing as an American poet had fallen drastically, I felt that there might be value in studying what had happened to the original *Double Axe* manuscript. Jeffers' philosophy, I found, not only caused him serious problems with his publisher over this volume, but it also affected the artistic quality of his poetry and, eventually, his reputation as a poet. My intent in this book, then, is to survey briefly Jeffers' philosophy and its genesis, to discuss the circumstances under which the original manuscript of the *Double Axe* went unpublished, and to explicate the unpublished poems and place them within the Jeffers canon, seeking thereby to reestablish a proper persective from which one may approach the poet.

Chapter 1, "A Kind of Awakening," traces the development of Jeffers' philosophy and poetry. His ideas grew out of his contradictory attitudes, as well as experiences in college, his marriage, and his early feelings of patriotism. He was especially influenced by World War I. As he formulated his philosophy, his ideas about the role that his poetry should play developed as well, beginning the chain of events that ultimately led to the deletion of ten poems from *The Double Axe*.

Chapter 2 is titled "The Will Is the Corruptor." For Jeffers the universe was one entity "out of grasp of the mind enormous." Its parts were only differing manifestations of a single energy; all bore upon and influenced one another. They changed, ceased to exist, and came into being. Nothing — stars, atoms, individuals, races, culture-ages — was important in itself; each was significant only as part of the universal totality. This entity, as a whole and in its parts, was beautiful and, according to Jeffers, should compel our deepest respect and love. In the final view *only* the whole could be beautiful, deserving of love, regarded and treated as divine. To Jeffers we who are human could attain true freedom and peace by loving this single wholeness, by turning away from self, mankind, human contrivances, imaginings, and dreams. World War II became a dramatic testing ground for this philosophy. The war reflected the inhumanism Jeffers considered as natural to man as the contention between the ocean and the rocks or between the hawk and the hare.

Inasmuch as the doctrine of inhumanism permeates Jeffers' poetry, the depth of his moral commitment and of his passionate intensity were profoundly tested by the American public, which reacted with hostility to the book. Did he dare treat the war as "natural"?

Chapter 3, "The Double Axe Murder," shows how, as a further consequence of Jeffers' unpopular doctrine, the text of *The Double Axe* was altered. Notes and letters from the period show that Bennett Cerf and Saxe Commins were disconcerted by the intensity and by some of the political ramifications of Jeffers' doctrine. Under their direction Random House assumed the role of guardian-censor for postwar America and removed ten poems from the original manuscript, making a number of changes in the remaining poems as well. The volume was finally printed without the most "offensive" poems and with a publisher's disclaimer regarding "the political views pronounced by the poet," but public response to Jeffers' views was antagonistic and reactionary nonetheless.

Chapter 4, "The Stones of Whiteness," offers close readings and analysis of the excised poems. In these poems the doctrine of inhumanism is stated most explicitly and perhaps, least poetically, but these poems also show the intensity of Jeffers' convictions.

Chapter 5, "The Parable of the Water," discusses why Jeffers deferred to editorial opinion and allowed the poems to be excised. Curiously, Jeffers reworked two of the poems that ultimately appeared in *The Double Axe*. My reading of them points up the artistic possibilities of the expunged poems.

Jeffers never extricated himself from the aesthetic predicament that his particularly dark philosophy brought about: years after *The Double Axe* controversy, in *Hungerfield,* the last book published during his lifetime, Saxe Commins again failed to see his art, although he remained intensely aware of the polemic.

FOREWORD

Robert J. Brophy

That Robinson Jeffers' *The Double Axe and Other Poems* was meant to be a very different book seems abundantly clear from James Shebl's recounting of "The Double Axe Murder." Reviewing the excised and the altered materials and then reconstructing in imagination the original text, the reader is left speechless at Random House's presumptuousness and at Jeffers' enigmatic acquiescence. True, the times were political and the publishers nervous. Ironically, however, Saxe Commins and Bennett Cerf seem only to have compounded the problem by their editorial interference. Jeffers' original preface, for instance, which Shebl makes available here for the first time, is in many ways a beautiful and reconciling context for the polemical poems to be presented. By precipitating Jeffers' withdrawal of the original preface and by inhibiting the intended flow of the poems, the editors produced a *more* polemical book, less aesthetically directed and unified—a work that *does* seem propagandistic because it is a collection of dislocated illustrations of a thesis that was never presented properly.

The original preface seems more a part of the work than does any Jeffers attempted elsewhere. It is as though it were a thesis or statement against which an antithesis might be set to arrive at a synthesis of reconciliation and wisdom, the antithesis being the human contortions dramatized in the poems. Lacking that preface, the reader is faced with Jeffers' isolated note on inhumanism, followed by an editor's disclaimer, and then with an abrupt entry into a series of poems that illustrate what never was allowed to be stated: how humankind, in various ways—now in the frivolity and foolishness of a postwar period, now in a crescendo of new war preparation, now in paroxysms of martial violence, now in delusions of victory—is the blind adolescent victim of its own folly and never learns from its history.

Human capability for violence is beyond understanding and control. This truth troubled Jeffers' poetic consciousness as early as the mid-twenties in "The Tower Beyond Tragedy," a verse parable similar in many ways to "The Double Axe," in which Jeffers argued noninvolvement in political dynamics for one compelling reason—its blinding, self-serving, quasi-idolatrous entrapment. Orestes, who culminates the drama's bloodletting with matricide, partly in the hope that a new, less repressive political order might emerge, says of this capability for compounded, senseless violence:

> *Here is the penalty:*
> *You gather up all your forces to the act, and afterward*
> *Silence, no voice, no ghost, vacancy, but all's not expended.*
> *Those powers want bitter action. No object.*
> *Deeds are too easy. Our victims are too fragile, they ought*
> *to have thousands of lives, you strike out once only*
> *The sky breaks like a bubble. . . .* (Selected Poetry, p. 130)

But the very monstrousness of his act proves to be a grace; Orestes is mercifully carried beyond guilt and further introvertive activity. The killing of his mother acts as a kind of electroshock therapy, shattering the human idols of his mind, driving him to the mountain, distraught but finally unfettered. His consciousness, after its troubled human interlude, expands cosmically till he can at last unite himself to the God of nature and of the whole inhuman universe.

In 1948, Mycenae was the United States of America, and the post-Trojan War's political paroxysms were World War II and its aftermath. Victors and vanquished were only pitiful, intent on learning nothing, satisfied with self-justification, hero-congratulation, recrimination toward enemies, and preparations for new wars. Not that far from Mycenae's victors and vanquished were Hitler and Truman, Mussolini and Roosevelt; the difference was merely a few cycles of history. Jeffers' *Double Axe* preface attempted to give the postwar world that insight, that "distancing" that might somehow justify the violence by sobering and detaching the "victors." This is why *The Double Axe* without its original preface is an argument without prologue, a truncated phone conversation in which the key initial words are cut off.

It might also be argued that the preface was an integral aesthetic part of the volume. Jeffers' custom in publishing was to offer a statement, usually dramatized in a long narrative poem, and to illustrate this theme in its various facets through the shorter poems. Jeffers' prose meditation in *The Double Axe* would have served this same theme-defining function. As it is, the substitute statement, Jeffers' "Preface" on inhumanism, appears to be an afterthought, an answer to the publisher instead of something that forms the original cast of the volume. And the publisher's interpolation that separates Jeffers' preface from its poems comes as a wrenching interruption, demanding that the volume be taken as vituperation, the misconceived rantings of one politically deranged. It sees and allows no aesthetic unity; it takes the poems as an assorted collection rather than a unity that was meant to illustrate the inhumanist viewpoint. The ramifications are profound: instead of concluding and perhaps reconciling philosophically a span of war poetry that began at least as far back as 1934, the 1948 volume was made into an isolated, distempered, sputtering episode. And as to Jeffers' reputation, who can say? Perhaps by reason of the misrepresentation he lost some readers, but he had few at the time. He was detached enough not to protest or even care. The real damage was done, however, in withholding the evidence of his artistic integrity from a later, more sympathetic and unbiased audience. It seems to have doomed Jeffers to undeserved misunderstanding and possible dismissal by a new generation of critics. *The Double Axe*, as published, has always been a stumbling block for friend or foe.

James Shebl brings his case and its evidence together effectively and lucidly. He is direct, precisely spoken, and single-minded. He does not grandly attempt to place Jeffers' war poems in a context with all the poet's other work; to do so would have been a distraction. He hardly pauses to decry the typical and perennial refusal of critics to receive the poet on his own terms, or to allow Jeffers to finish speaking before they interrupt with their annoyances and glib dismissals. The present volume gains dignity for this reserve. Shebl's refutation of the critics is everywhere implicit and devastating. His point, his thesis, his intent is simple enough: to demonstrate that Jeffers is characteristically misconstrued by those (this time, his editors) who do not listen to his sentence to the end. In this study of the editing fiasco of *The Double Axe,* Shebl offers us a paradigm by which to understand Jeffers' whole critical reception. If those most sympathetic, who professed their pride in him, were so out of touch and so arrogantly self-assured, what could be expected from his detractors?

IN THIS
WILD
WATER

1.

A KIND OF
AWAKENING

When Random House published *The Double Axe and Other Poems* in 1948,[1] it included on the dust jacket as well as following the author's preface, a publisher's disclaimer noting the controversial nature of the poetry within. Except for the publication and subsequent production of the highly acclaimed adaptation of Euripides' *Medea* in 1946, this book constituted the printed poetic efforts of Robinson Jeffers following World War II.

The Double Axe contained much of what was integral to the Jeffers canon: an unorthodox treatment of familial ties, religion, nature, and society and the poet's condemnation of humanity because of man's behavior and cultural mores. To him, man was but a piece of matter and of no special concern to God. Jeffers celebrated, rather, a cosmic unity, beyond man, speaking of one existence, one music, one organism, one life, one God,[2]

Not a tribal nor an anthropoid God.
Not a ridiculous projection of human fears,
needs, dreams,
justice and love lust.

And from his early to his later poetry, Robinson Jeffers had indeed treated man as decidedly less important, showing instead a preoccupation with landscape. But although many of Jeffers' early poems addressed the problems of "transient civilization," it was not until the forties that his verse moved from direct concern with nature and became increasingly propagandistic. He began to incorporate in his poetry contemporary issues and political figures to articulate his dark view of man.

There was little in Jeffers' early life, however, to suggest that such stern naturalism eventually would come from his pen. Although his family moved often when he was a child, he was well adjusted and well liked when he entered Occidental College at the age of 16. As one of his biographers, Melba Berry Bennett, noted:[3]

Although only sixteen, Robin was so advanced in his studies that he was given junior standing at Occidental. But this apparently was not held against him by his classmates and it didn't take him long, in spite of his diffidence, to enter into the activities of his class. Neither aggressiveness nor an acute social sense was a necessary tool with which to make friendships in this small college. A similarity of tastes was all that was required to become one with this group whose members were as steeped in the classics as was Robin. They had as serious an approach to their weekend hikes and athletics as to their academic studies. These associations and circumstances were ideal for Robin's development. He felt no self-consciousness and, instead of solitary excursions, he

4

joined the other students on weekend trips to the mountains and nearby canyons. He quickly gained in popularity and soon became known as "Jeff" to his intimates. His inner freedom developed, and he wrote more poetry.

According to Bennett, Jeffers was quite at home with the way of life at Occidental College. He was a well-traveled student, a member of the track team, and an outdoors enthusiast who demonstrated a Spartan stamina and a sensitivity for natural delights — trees, flowers, birds, and rocks.

In June of 1904, Jeffers received his bachelor's degree, and the following year he enrolled at the University of Southern California for graduate study. There, he met Mrs. Una Call Kuster, a fellow student. Although initially only friends, their attraction quickly grew. At first, students and faculty at USC encouraged the friendship, for they saw Una as a steadying influence on Robin, who had turned to writing poems all night, "fortified with a jug of wine, a packet of Bull Durham, and a sheaf of cigarette papers." But during the summer of 1908, Robin and Una exchanged innumerable love letters testifying to their illicit love. They began meeting clandestinely, and the gossip began. In something of a scandal, Una obtained a divorce, and they married on August 2, 1913.[4]

When rumors of war were confirmed in September 1914, Robin and Una were forced to give up plans they had made to live in England. A family friend told them of "a little village called Carmel, near the historical old town of Monterey. . . . It was this little village, with its blue sea, its pine forests, and fearsome, jagged coast-range, to which Robin and Una Jeffers came."[5]

As the 1914 war mushroomed, the poet was caught up with the sense of responsibility that many young nationalists were beginning to feel. Jeffers was anxious to "enlist in his country's service." As he later wrote,[6]

5

As to my motives in offering (rather late) to become a soldier: I did feel a duty to protect the country that had protected me and my few possessions . . . . On the other hand I felt a duty to stay home and help take care of year old sons . . . I had no conscientious objection to fighting; it seems to me a natural condition of the race. But I was never deluded with ideas of a noble or crusading war; it seems to me an unavoidable spectacular madness.

Throughout the call for troops my mind was perplexed and at conflict with itself. I felt quite sure that this conflict emotionally realized the external world for me and made much of the difference between my verses before the war and my verses since.

Jeffers felt that he had "a duty to protect the country that had protected him and his few possessions," but at the same time he was confused. It was not simply a conscientious patriotism that he felt; some deeper understanding, a philosophic attitude, contributed to his mixed feelings. Combat, he sensed, was natural to man. This observation—his recognition of man's animalistic tendencies—was the beginning of the development of Jeffers' view. Produced by the character of World War I and the personal tension he felt, Jeffers' embryonic form of inhumanism, as he came to call his philosophy, was beginning to take shape. Later, writing in the third person in an autobiographical note, he reflected that[7]

he (Jeffers) regards war with horror and disgust but believes it to be inevitable—and claims that he sees, at a certain level of contemplation, the tragic and the spectacular beauty of war, as of a storm or other natural disaster.

He came to believe, then, that not only was war intrinsic to man, but it was natural per se, a part of *everything* natural.

6

Letters to his friends, odd bits of autobiographical commentary still in manuscript form, and sketches of poems that were never published document the evolution of Jeffers' view. But his ideas did not develop without internal or personal tension, deliberations, and conflict. Because he felt that his wife, Una, was like a part of him, he was dismayed when she refused to consent to his intention to enlist. For her to discourage his engaging in a cause for which he had a strong natural inclination seemed contradictory. As "part" of him, she should share his ideas.

Throughout their life together, Una had assumed the role of protectress;[8] she seemed to appreciate Jeffers' destiny to announce and defend man's perpetual self-struggle. And, as he habitually deferred to her protectiveness, one can well imagine Jeffers' dilemma when he entered into negotiations with the armed forces to offer his services, despite Una's express disapproval.

A number of brief notes to Jeffers from the War Department, in the Jeffers Collection at the University of Texas, trace the poet's negotiations and reveal his vacillation. It appears that, following his own feelings exclusively, he volunteered for service; he was directed to respond by January 2, 1917, with "draft data necessary for induction."[9] Then, in reply to this order, Jeffers filed a claim for exemption, Una apparently having changed his mind:

ANSWERING QUESTIONNAIRE, DECEMBER 31, I CLAIMED DEFERRED CLASSIFICATION (CLASS IV) ON ACCOUNT OF DEPENDENT WIFE AND TWO CHILDREN, CLAIM STILL PENDING.

Despite this claim for exemption, which eventually was granted, Jeffers changed his mind again and a few days later volunteered his services in aviation:

7

JANUARY 5, 1918. FROM THE AVIATION EXAMINING BOARD: DISCONTINUANCE OF APPLICATIONS FOR BALLOON DIVISION, IN THE SIGNAL OFFICERS' RESERVE CORPS. SUGGEST AMENDING APPLICATION TO READ "PILOT."

On January 5, 1918, Jeffers received his notice of Classification IV from the Monterey County Selective Service Board in Salinas; and then, on January 17, 1918, from the Aviation Examining Board came a request for clarification, noting that:

APPLICATION FOR COMMISSION INDICATES SOME QUESTION IN JEFFERS' MIND AS TO HIS "UNDERSTANDING OF THE TERM 'PILOT.'"

A subsequent ruling denied his request to be considered as a pilot:

IT IS TO BE REGRETTED THAT THE FACT THAT YOU HAVE REACHED YOUR THIRTY-FIRST YEAR EXCLUDES A CHANGE OF YOUR APPLICATION AT THE PRESENT TIME TO THAT OF "PILOT."

So, he tried again:

JANUARY 21, 1918. FROM THE AVIATION EXAMINING BOARD: APPLICATION FOR ADMISSION. BOARD IS NOT AUTHORIZED TO EXAMINE AT PRESENT ANY APPLICANTS FOR SERVICE AS AERIAL OBSERVERS.

On January 25, 1918, he was successful in getting himself reclassified, and he received notice of his Classification I. The final verdict came November 15, 1918, after armistice had been declared:[10]

FROM DIRECTOR OF MILITARY AERONAUTICS, RE DISQUALIFI-
CATION: BOARD BEFORE WHICH YOU RECENTLY APPEARED FOR
THE PURPOSE OF DETERMINING YOUR QUALIFICATIONS FOR
COMMISSION IN THE AIR SERVICE (AERONAUTICS) HAS REPORTED
UNFAVORABLY.

As cryptic as these governmental documents are, they
suggest the predicament that Jeffers created for himself: while
answering a questionnaire necessary to acquire a deferred
classification (December 31, 1917), he was negotiating with
the Signal Officer's Reserve Corps (January 5, 1918).

In an autobiographical holograph, probably written as
preparation for answering a letter or questionnaire,[11] Jeffers
explained his ambivalent behavior. In third person, he
drafted (and revised) his recollections:[12]

> It seemed to him that war was unavoidable as the world was
> (and is) arranged. He thought in 1916 that our entrance
> into the war on one side or the other was unavoidable. (Is
> not so sure of that now.) Disliked the cant of our neutrality,
> followed by the cant of ~~"our-war-for-democracy"~~ ~~"war-to-
> end-war,~~" our belligerancy [*sic*].

> Did not enlist in the ranks because we were very poor,
> seemed to have no financial future, and had two babies.
> <u>Suffered</u> <u>considerable</u> <u>disturbance</u> <u>of</u> <u>mind</u> <u>on</u> <u>the</u> <u>subject</u>.
> Made various unsuccessful applications for training for
> commission—examined for aviation, rejected on account of
> high blood pressure.

> ~~Disturbance of mind and~~ <u>Conflict</u> <u>of</u> <u>motives</u> <u>on</u> <u>the</u> <u>subject</u> <u>of</u>
> <u>going</u> <u>to</u> <u>war</u> <u>or</u> <u>not</u> <u>was</u> <u>probably</u> <u>one</u> <u>of</u> <u>several</u> <u>factors</u> <u>that</u>
> <u>about</u> <u>this</u> <u>time</u> <u>made</u> <u>the</u> <u>world</u> <u>and</u> <u>his</u> <u>own</u> <u>mind</u> <u>much</u>
> <u>more</u> <u>real</u> <u>and</u> <u>intense</u> <u>to</u> <u>him</u>. ~~A kind of awakening~~ So that
> he felt at the age of thirty-one a kind of awakening, such
> as adolescents and religious converts are said to experience.

9

In these notes Jeffers recorded his early philosophic development. Evolving from his seemingly tranquil life at Occidental,
his early feelings of patriotism, his growing belief in the
naturaliness of war, and even his submission to Una's
protective guidance, Jeffers' philosophy of inhumanism ger-
minated in the intensity of his contradictory experiences and
attitudes. Then, at the age of thirty-one came the almost
religious awakening, followed by the formulation of the stark
doctrine that his poetry was to illustrate.

If Jeffers could accept the naturalness of war philosophically, he could not condone men's general folly: the indisputable
conceit of the race that proclaimed harmony even as it
practiced hostility. The brutality of war would be found
increasingly well represented in prose, Jeffers felt, but not in
the symbolist or imagist poetry popular at the time. In the
foreword to *The Selected Poetry of Robinson Jeffers* (1937),[13]
Jeffers wrote that

> poetry—if it was to survive at all—must reclaim some of the
> power and reality that it was so hastily surrendering to
> prose. The modern French poetry of the time, and the most
> "modern" of the English poetry, seem[s] to me thoroughly
> defeatist. It [is] becoming slight and fantastic, abstract,
> unreal, eccentric; and [is] not even saving its soul, for these
> are generally anti-poetic qualities. It must reclaim sub-
> stance and sense, and physical and psychological reality.

Much of the poetry Jeffers wrote during these years shows that
he was indeed exploring the "physical and psychological
reality" he called for. Responding to Nietzsche's comment,
"The Poets? The poets lie too much," Jeffers acknowledged his
sympathies with the poet who spoke the brutal truth about
man's natural state.[14]

I decided not to tell lies in verse. Not to feign any emotion I did not feel; not to pretend to believe in optimism or pessimism or irreversible progress; not to say anything because it was popular, or generally accepted, or fashionable in intellectual circles, unless I myself believed it; and not to believe easily. These negatives limit the field; I am not recommending them but for my own occasions.

It was this uncompromising commitment to speak the truth at whatever cost that at once gave Jeffers his integrity as a man and a poet and yet caused him much anxiety. It was one thing to speak one's mind if the message was warm and favorable; it was another thing to speak a message like Jeffers'.

In *Themes in My Poems* Jeffers delineated the world view that informed his poetry. The universe, in all of its fragmentation, he believed, is one; "a being 'out of grasp of the mind enormous.'"[15] Each of the constituent parts of the universe functions in a relationship to the others; only the totality is important. The oneness alone—contrary to man's wishes and narcissism—is divine. This is the truth that the poet must speak. Man must be persuaded to see his own relative insignificance. Humanity, Jeffers said, is but "a moving lichen / On the cheek of the round stone."[16] The step necessary for man to obtain a correct perspective of himself is for him to "find the secure value / The all-heal [Jeffers] found when a former time hurt [him] / to the heart, / The splendor of inhuman things."[17] Such a message required a forceful, and perhaps offending, strategy.

The approach that Jeffers took was to employ particulars as metaphors; he used well-known people to illustrate his philosophy. In his hands this topicality caused some very serious problems. Because he used celebrated contemporaries to articulate his ideas, nearly every reference to a living person had the effect of an indictment. But this approach was not new. James Joyce, W. B. Yeats, and even Dante referred to politicians and other public figures of their day. In much the same way, Jeffers used Roosevelt, Truman, Hitler, and Stalin as specific metaphors to give his poetry immediacy.[18]

> *the cripple's-power-need of Roosevelt; the*
> *bombast of Mussolini; the tinsel star of Napoleon.*

And also in "The Love and the Hate":[19]

> *The boiler of life and death: you can see faces;*
> *there's Tojo, there's Roosevelt.*

These people represented certain ideas and attitudes that Jeffers sought to work with. Roosevelt's crippled figure, for example, embodied what he saw as Roosevelt's (and Hitler's and Jeanne d'Arc's and Napoleon's) limited and deformed view of men, nations, and civilization itself. To the reader Jeffers may have seemed to be taking advantage of—or even ridiculing—Roosevelt's physical handicap. But when Jeffers did not include such references, his poetry became especially propagandist and cerebral. Consider the following poem, untitled and (no doubt wisely) unpublished.[20]

Untitled Poem

We see ourselves from within, our minds and senses
Observe our own minds and senses
> *We see the universe from within, we are little parts of it;*
> *no astronomer*
Ever knew the stars from outside the stars. All our knowledge then,
Our opinions, our observations, our science,
Are subjective, are sometimes studying itself
By the light of itself. That is to say that all our knowledge is a
> *dream dreaming: say rather a dream*

12

Dreaming a dream.
But we must dream it whole: that way lies truth.
We must not say in Berkeley's answer that I am real
And the world is my dream; that's darkness,
I'm only as real as a wave of the sea.
I am the sea.
  Don't fool yourself: there is reality
Under the dream: if I dream it whole and not in fragments
    nor contradictions,
I shall approach reality. This is called truth. The truth's the
    dream
That comes nearest the real:—and we must trust our truth,
We have nothing better. No doubt at all there are huge gaps in it;
    but there's nothing
Consciously false.
  Very well: what enlarges truth? Experience.
For truth must grow or die. Truth, like all vital things—
When our bodies or minds or truth stop growing,
There begins death.
    Experience. What kind of experience?
What kind of experience?
I am fifty years old; I am too old to take intelligently
    the limited experience
Of an observatory or laboratory: truth's little workshops, but
    how limited!—and those people
Tell us their findings.
   As for me: to take what comes:
  not to withdraw from any experience
An old man finds.
  I have seen over the edge once or twice, at least I
    thought so:
  keep my mind open for it
I will again. I must find experience never known in my past
    and let it free
Some gaps in truth.

Although the poem offers a dialectic of ideas and perhaps could be regarded as something like an interior monologue, in which a persona deliberates within himself and tries to arrive at some acceptable understanding of the meaning and significance of experience, such a view would overlook the absence of concrete images and metaphors, the rambling and unshaped form, the preachy and arrogant tone, and the failure of the words to reach any universal significance. It is, in short, an expository meditation in the guise of a poem. It should be remembered, however, that Jeffers probably recognized these failings of this work, for he never offered it for publication.

But on occasion, especially during the war, Jeffers did write and attempt to publish poems quite similar to this one. The reason for this kind of propagandist poetry was that it seemed to him[21]

> that *great poetry* gathers and expresses the whole of things, as prose *never can*. Its business is to contain a whole world at once, the physical and the sensuous, the intellectual, the spiritual, the imaginative, all in one passionate solution. Thus it becomes a means of discovery, as well as a means of expression. Science usually takes things to pieces in order to discover them; it dissects and analyzes; poetry puts things together, producing equally valid discovery, and actual creation. Something new is found out, something that the author himself did not know before he wrote it; and something new is made.

The discovery that Jeffers sought in his poetry was the discovery of inhumanism. He sought to articulate a way by which man could come to realize his role in the universe, and poetry was primarily the medium he used. When he avoided

14

concrete and metaphorical particulars, his poetry became little more than a statement of doctrine. Because Jeffers' poems dealt with value and perspective, one did not necessarily experience a new or revealing sensation, but rather encountered Jeffers' perception of man's place in the universe.

Hitler, Roosevelt, and World War II gave him new ideas, as well as reinforced his old ones. In the original preface for *The Double Axe* (set aside after the publisher's decision to print a disclaimer) Jeffers wrote of man's excessive energies, which he felt, led man to superfluous activities—activities[22] that were "devoted to self-interference, self-frustration, self-incitement and self-worship."

> The waste is enormous. We are able to commit and endure because we are so firmly established on the planet. Life is actually so easy that it requires only a slight fraction of our common energies. The rest we discharge onto each other in conflict and charity, love, jealousy, hatred, competition, government, vanity and cruelty and that puerile passion, the will to power or for amusement. Certain human relationships are necessary and desirable but not to this extent. This is a kind of collective onanism; pathetic and ridiculous or at noblest, tragic incest. And so I have represented it. But we have all this excess energy. What should we do with it? . . . Do I really believe that people will be content to take a walk and admire the beauty of things? Certainly not. I'm speaking of a racial disease. It was in the monkey blood we derived from and no doubt it is incurable. But whoever will can minimize it in his own life.

In the unpublished draft Jeffers described the content of the book as representing "a new manner of thought and feeling which came to [him] at the end of the war of 1914."[23]

It is based on the recognition of the astonishing beauty of things and on a rational acceptance of the fact that mankind is neither central nor important in the universe.

And in Section 45 of Part II of *The Double Axe*, Jeffers poeticized this idea: "Love man in God," for God "is rock, earth and water, and / the beasts and stars; and the night that contains / them. A day will come when the earth / will scratch herself and smile and rub off humanity . . . ." Jeffers then addressed the future children of the race, telling them not to cry, for they were but temporarily born to earth.[24]

> *And when your death-day comes do not weep; you are*
> *   not going far.*
> *You are going to your better nature, the nobler*
> *   elements, earth, air and water.*

In his later poems Jeffers grappled with this reading of man's nature. He wrote to discover a way to minimize this "racial disease." In doing so, he found it necessary to illustrate the sickness of civilization with specific examples. Thus, he dramatically compared the American and the German or Roosevelt and Hitler and ultimately offended the sensibilities (and patriotism) of Random House and its readers.

Jeffers asked of his readers a difficult task: to relate the experience of the poem, distinctive and irreducible, to the larger flow of human experience. Such a challenge required that the reader be sensitive not only to Jeffers' specific point in a particular poem but to the history of human development and, beyond that, to the evolution of the natural universe. In his poems, that is, Jeffers would ask the reader to consider his, and even mankind's, smallness in the immense context of the development of the universe. Poetry for Jeffers was not merely mimetic or ontological but polemical as well. His poems were not necessarily or always tracts, but the materials on which they were based and the criteria by which the poet organized them were frequently the same as those found in religious or philosophical statements. In one sense, it might be said that Jeffers elevated propaganda to art by making poetry out of the stuff of argument. But in another sense, Jeffers' best poems carried an autonomy and distinctiveness that made them irreducible; they could not be completely understood by deciphering the polemic that pointed back to external, contemporary reality. His poetry built and inhabited a world of its own. Thus, the statements in a Jeffers poem could not be understood or judged as if they had been made in direct speech, for when his aesthetic served him best, it had its own complicating norms and dramatic justifications.

In an unpublished preface written for *Tamar* in August 1923,[25] Jeffers spoke of poetry "as presenting the universal beauty," thus being "an incitement to life." He wrote that "poetry in its higher condition is . . . an incitement to action, because our actions are a part of that beauty; an incitement to contemplation, because it serves to open our intelligence and senses to that beauty. . . . This poetry must be rhythmic, and must deal with permanent things, and must avoid affectation." Because Jeffers believed conflict and political deceit to be conditions of man, he considered them permanent and dealt with them as realities in his poetry. He even incorporated specific references to persons or events that he felt exemplified these conditions. And yet he spoke of "the passionate present-ment of beauty which is poetry's function." Far from being mere political dogma, Jeffers' poetry had an artistic autonomy; it served an artistic function. The particulars he employed were intended to point up a "permanent human faculty," and thus were both real and poetic. When he did not use particulars, he sacrificed not only the reality but the poetry.

But artistically presented or not, Jeffers' ideas offended many, and the public outcry against them eventually put his convictions to the test.

2.

THE WILL IS THE CORRUPTER

Eagle and Hawk with their great claws and hooked heads
  tear life to pieces;
Vluture and raven wait for death to soften it.
The poet cannot feed on this time of the world
Until he has torn it to pieces,
  and himself also.

"Tear Life to Pieces"
(The Beginning and the End)

As early as 1939, Jeffers had discovered in the word
inhuman a referential concept to describe the meaning of
Hitler and of his own poetry: both warned against themselves.
In "The Day is a Poem," written on September 19 of that year,[1]
Jeffers developed a theme suggested by a newscast announcing
Hitler's success in Danzig:

> *Well: the day is a poem: but too much*
> *like one of Jeffers', crusted with blood and barbaric*
>   *omens,*
> *Painful to excess, inhuman as a hawk's cry.*

In his admission of being "painful to excess," Jeffers pointed out that the horrible message of Hitler's success was not unlike that of his own poetry: that war and brutality were natural to man; man himself was inhumane. Although poking fun at himself in a rather macabre way, he acknowledged the harsh implications of his poetry, and in the phrase "crusted with blood," he admitted to having actually inflicted wounds.

Especially interesting was the simile Jeffers used to embody the abstract concept of inhumanism: the hawk's cry. In selecting the hawk, Jeffers joined proud, fierce strength with the instincts for attack and freedom and pointed symbolically to his poetry as a proud, lofty cry of attack. It was mundane in subject and sublime in expectation; it was dissociated from man, although it cried to him, just as a hawk's cry might be interpreted as a scream of pain, warning, or acknowledgment.

And Jeffers' special philosophy required a powerful cry to make it heard, because to Jeffers man appeared so unaware of his nature. He felt that man regarded himself as a warm, compassionate and superior creature, immune to natural pressures. The hawk, and for that matter, Hitler, would show him to be otherwise. And so should a poet of integrity. Jeffers' approach was, therefore, marked by a predilection for subjects like death, war, and rise and decline of cultures, and naturalism. And yet Jeffers himself was neither Hitler nor hawk; he belonged to the society he sought to awaken. His art was grounded in his sympathetic experience as a man; yet as a poet he had to remain apart and urge man to seek an objective and detached perspective.

Jeffers counseled:[2]

Turn away from each other to that great presence to which humanity is only a squirming particle. Love your neighbor as yourself, that is, not excessively if you are adult and normal, but God with all your heart and mind and soul. Turn outward from each other as far as need and kindness permit to the vast life and inexhaustible beauty beyond humanity. This is not a slight matter but an essential condition of freedom and of moral and of final sanity. It is understood that this attitude is peculiarly unacceptable at the present, being opposed not only by egoism and tradition but by all the currents of the moment. We are now completely trapped in the nets of envy, intrigue, corruption, compulsion, and eventual murder that are called international politics. We have always been expansive, predatory and missionary; and we love to lie to ourselves. We have entered the period of civil struggles and emerging Caesarism that binds republics with brittle iron. Civilization everywhere is in its age of decline and abnormal violence. Men are going to be frightened and herded increasingly into lumps and masses. A frightened man cannot think and the mass mind does not want truth, only democratic or Aryan or Marxian or other colored truth. It wants its own voices. However, the truth will not die and persons who have lost everything in the culmination of these evils and stand beyond hope and almost beyond fear may find it again. But if in some future age, the dreams of Utopia should incredibly be fulfilled and men were actually free of want and fear, then all the more they would need this sanctuary against the deadly emptiness, and insignificance of their lives at leisure fully realized. Man much more than baboon or wolf is an animal formed for conflict. His life seems to be meaningless without it. Only a clear shift of meaning and emphasis from man to not-man can make him whole.

Jeffers believed that this manner of thought and feeling involved no "falsehoods," and that it had "objective truth and human value." It offered "a reasonable detachment as a rule of conduct, instead of love, hate and envy." He felt that inhumanism neutralized "fanaticism and wild hopes"; but it provided "magnificence for the religious instinct," and satisfied our "need to admire greatness and rejoice in beauty."[3] If Jeffers' poetry was to articulate this "truth," its powers would indeed be tested, for he was asking that his verse completely redirect man's attention and concern.

In 1951, Jeffers' response to a request from the American Humanist Association for an application of the term *humanist* to his philosophy, was published in *The Humanist*. In the section designated "Ambiguous or Equivocal," Jeffers wrote briefly:[4]

March 25, 1951

The word Humanism refers primarily to the Renaissance interest in art and literature rather than in theological doctrine; and personally I am content to leave it there. "Naturalistic Humanism"—in the modern sense—is no doubt a better philosophical attitude than many others, but the emphasis seems wrong; "human naturalism" would seem to me more satisfactory, with but little accent on the "human." Man is a part of nature, but a nearly infinitesimal part; the human race will cease after a while and leave no trace, but the great splendors of nature will go on. Meanwhile most of our time and energy are necessarily spent on human affairs; that can't be prevented, though I think it should be minimized; but for philosophy, which is an endless research of the truth, and for contemplation, which can be a sort of worship, I would suggest that the immense beauty of the earth and the outer universe, the divine "nature of things," is a more rewarding object. Certainly it is more ennobling. It is a source of strength; the other of distraction.

24

But if Jeffers would remind man of his smallness, he would also remind him of the great splendor of nature. As Lawrence Clark Powell wrote in *Robinson Jeffers: The Man and His Work:*[5]

> A fertile gift of image making, together with a ranging imagination which sees present phenomena in the light of a long evolution, make his verse often unmistakable. . . . This imagination, fortified by a knowledge of history and science, leads Jeffers to a vision of the vast universe of astrophysics, in which man is an essential, ephemeral part. . . . He holds our civilization to be decadent, centered only in itself and in its anthropocentric universe; and that wars and vice are undermining it, and the whole structure doomed to dissolve in ruins. Though he is not a reformer he has a message to the world, which is for men to turn from self-worship to a recognition of the greater inhuman universe.

It is at this point that many critics limit Jeffers' meaning of inhumanism. They see Jeffers' repudiation of human self-aggrandizement but often fail to see his almost pantheistic admiration of the "greater inhuman universe." Citing Jeffers' prefatory statement in *The Double Axe,* which describes inhumanism as a "shifting emphasis from man to not-man," Mercedes Cunningham Monjian, for example, recognized the implications of inhumanism as a negative humanism that "denies" man's interests and development, subduing them in the interests of something greater.[6] But Monjian's emphasis led her to assert incorrectly that "all of Jeffers' poetry demonstrated this denial of man's importance and potential." Far from a philosophy of denial like Puritanism, it was, rather, a philosophy of perspective. Man had a role to play in

the universe; it might not be as important as man usually
regarded it, but it was not unimportant. Man must see himself
from the universal perspective of time and space:[7]

> *Galaxy on galaxy, innumerable swirls of*
>   *unnumerable stars,*
>   *endured as it were forever and humanity*
> *Came into being, its two or three million years*
>   *are but a moment, in a moment it*
>   *will certainly cease out from being*
> *And galaxy on galaxy endure after that as it*
>   *were forever*
> *. . . But man is conscious.*
>   *He brings the world to focus in a feeling brain,*
> *In a net of nerves catches the splendor of*
>   *things,*
> *Breaks the somnambulism of nature . . . His*
>   *distinction perhaps,*
> *Hardly his advantage.*

But man brought consciousness to nature; he could recognize
the splendor of it all, even though he himself was only a small
and ephemeral part of it. Although, as Jeffers suggested, man
"breaks the somnambulism of nature," he could not use his
distinctive consciousness decisively to alter nature to his
advantage. This idea, of course, ran counter to human wish
and narcissism and to man's definition of progress — which
often placed man teleologically on top of the final heap.
Emphatically, Jeffers begged for the repudiation of self-flat-
tering egotism:[8]

> *You had to fetch me out of the*
> *happy hill of not-being. Pfah, to hug a woman*
> *And make this I. That's the evil in the world, that letter.*
> *I—I. . . .*

To be sure, Jeffers believed in change and in evolution. He felt that all things contributed to the integrity of the evolving and continuing whole. Because man existed, he was essential to the evolution. Man's contribution was, however, of the same spirit (though not necessarily to the same degree) as that of other living things. His combativeness, his inhumanity, was as much a part of his contribution as was his humanness, his harmoniousness. As Jeffers saw it, the evolutionary process would someday (some era) bypass man; humanity would "certainly cease out from being," and things would still continue, as splendid and miraculous as ever, though there would be no consciousness to perceive it.

So Jeffers opted for a certain passivity. In *The Heel of Elohim,* Hyatt Howe Waggoner tried to draw a logical conclusion from what he saw as Jeffers' world view:[9]

> What Mr. Jeffers has lately taken to calling his "inhuman-ism" calls for just one thing, silence — as, indeed, Mr. Jeffers has recognized in "Margrave" and elsewhere:
>
> *I also am not innocent*
> *Of contagion, but have spread my spirit on the*
>   *deep world.*
> *I have gotten sons and sent the fire wider. . . .*
> *And have widened in my idleness*
> *The disastrous personality of life with poems.*

Indeed, Jeffers considered the possibility of silence and the consequences of spreading his spirit — in having "gotten sons and sent the fire wider" Jeffers seemed to have regretted his complicity in perpetuating the human contribution to the evolving whole. And yet, in his best-known poem, "Shine Perishing Republic," Jeffers acknowledged that he could not escape the process: "I sadly smiling remember that the flower fades to make fruit, the fruit rots to make earth." If he would

27

be tempted periodically to absolute silence, he nevertheless spoke, in "Boats in a Fog," of "the essential reality / Of creatures going about their business among the equally / Ernest elements of nature." So, too, must man go about his business, petty and inconsequential though it was when seen from Jeffers' perspective.

Radcliffe Squires studied Jeffers' ideas on the seeming devolution of man — the "disastrous personality of life." He found that in *Roan Stallion* inhumanism seemed, at least incidentally, to pose a solution to the problem of decadence. As Jeffers "became more certain," in Squires' words, of the implication of inhumanism,[10]

> it became more necessary to stack up the details of a violent nature in order to support his feeling that to live meaningfully one must withdraw from the ordinary ambitions of life.

Like Waggoner, Squires suspected that Jeffers would have had us "deny [ourselves] in order to restore [ourselves]."[11] Restraint, according to Squires, was the iron from which the steel of inhumanism was wrought. From Squires' point of view, Jeffers seemed to desire that men behave not like beasts but like beings capable of controlling instinct. Whereas Waggoner saw inhumanism as encouraging absolute passivity, Squires saw it as a doctrine of reasoned modification.[12] Reason, however, could give man only perspective, not restoration of a lost divinity or potency. If man's rational faculties, his consciousness, constituted his distinctiveness, that hardly served to his advantage. If properly (which is to say objectively) developed, reason might enable man to see his small and ephemeral place in the evolving cosmos, but it would not rescue him from that place or from its consequences.

Robinson Jeffers argued this position in most of his poems, though more specifically and emphatically in some than in others. In "The Place For No Story," for example, he wrote of the pastoral life, and its tranquility. At the end of the poem he reflected that "no imaginable / Human presence here could do anything / But dilute the lonely self-watchful passion."[13] A human presence, it seems, would offer little to the pastoral place because man measured his reality in terms of himself. Instead of seeing nature as an objective and peaceful system, he tended to see it anthropocentrically. He diluted the "passion" of that which was suprahuman. Jeffers instead would "praise life, it deserves praise,"[14] but all life, not just human. In "Signpost" he urged man to "turn right away from humanity," to love "things which are so beautiful" and that "are the God." In direct opposition to Waggoner's claim, Jeffers wrote that man would see that humanity had "a place under heaven." In growing to God — the universe and its many elements — men were "free, even to become human."[15] So, Jeffers felt, man could not realize what *he currently believed* to be his nature and still assume his true place, for what man now believed about himself and his powers would get in the way of his seeing and acknowledging his proper place. Man must proportion his desires to his true abilities; he must find and face the correct, unflattering perspective of himself.

Jeffers' work expressly articulated this perspective. In the note introducing *Be Angry At The Sun*,[16] Jeffers lamented,

> the obsession with contemporary history that pins many of [his] pieces to the calendar, like butterflies to cardboard. Poetry is not private monologue, but . . . it is not public speech either; and in general it is the worse for being timely. . . .

> Yet it is right that a man's views be expressed, though the poetry suffer for it. Poetry should represent the whole mind; if part of the mind is occupied unhappily, so much the worse. And no use postponing the poetry to a time when

these storms may have passed, for [he] think[s] we have but seen a beginning of them; the calm to look for is the calm at the whirlwind's heart.

The difficulties that readers may have with Jeffers' view stem, perhaps, not so much from a lack of understanding of Jeffers' inhumanism as from a confusion that occurs when his philosophy is illustrated poetically. Introspection, which inhumanism decries, was at best dangerous, Jeffers would have said, for it usually led to self-delusion or narcissism. Jeffers asked his readers poetically not to be "deluded by dreams . . . of universal justice or happiness." He argued that great civilizations had "broken down into violence . . . many times before" and that man must strive either to avoid such violence "with honor or [to] choose the least ugly faction." So to strive would be somewhat less an impossible or immoral effort than it might seem, because these evils were "essential." Jeffers rationalized the dilemma of trying to avoid violence while maintaining a sense of honor or deliberately choosing the "least ugly faction," by stating that no matter "however ugly" the parts appeared, the whole remained beautiful.[17]

> *Man dissevered from the earth and stars*
> *and his history . . . for contemplation or in fact . . .*
> *Often appears atrociously ugly. Integrity is wholeness,*
> *the greatest beauty is*
> *Organic wholeness, the wholeness of life and things,*
> *the divine beauty of the universe. Love that,*
> *not man*
> *Apart from that. . . .*

It was man alone—apart from the organic wholeness of the universe—that Jeffers warned against. He felt that the human race spent "Too much emotion on itself," had too much narcissism.[18]

The happiest and freest man is the scientist investigating nature, or the artist admiring it; the person who is interested in things that are not human. Or if he is interested in human things, let him regard them objectively, as a small part of the great music. Certainly humanity has claims on all of us; we can best fulfill them by keeping our emotional sanity; and this by seeing beyond and around the human race.

Inhumanism, then, was a philosophy asking for a perspective of detachment, and for man's acceptance of his relatively minor role. It called neither for man's repudiation of himself nor his determination to gain lost powers. Inhumanism may well have been a misunderstood word, loaded as it was with antihumanist connotations. The doctrine was, in effect, a suprahumanism that preached the oneness of the universe.

It asserted that each constituent part drew nurture and encouragement from the others, though sooner or later each might actively contend with the others in some necessary way, each partook of and contributed to the integrity of the whole. This total integrity, given the self-interested desires of man, was continuously being denied or ignored by man, who would subordinate the stars, the oceans, and the hawks to his own well-being. As man often would have it, morality was what benefited the human family. As Jeffers would have it, morality protected the integrity of the whole, at whatever expense to man or any other item within it.

Seeking desperately to illustrate what man did to himself when he denied his subordinate place in the totality, Jeffers often may have seemed to overillustrate his case, peopling his poetry with grotesque and objectionable human characters while he treated nonhuman things with reverence. Jeffers' position did not flatter man, and his message was difficult for people to hear. His was a corrective vision, and his poetry remained, in a large sense, offending.

In Jeffers' mind the correct perspective was calming and reasoned, and he sought to enable man to achieve it. He felt that the human will was the corrupter, for by its powers man aggrandized himself at the expense of his natural harmony with nature and the universe.

These were the motives behind Jeffers' poetry. And his was an especially dangerous art, for he would direct it to influence and reflect the reader's experience. Ultimately, perhaps the doctrine of inhumanism proved too challenging, doctrinaire, and unflattering to succeed as poetic material.

3.

THE DOUBLE AXE MURDER

As the McCarthy hearings later demonstrated in the fifties, America's success in World War II generated strong nationalistic feelings among some persons. It was not popular to find fault with the nation, and those people who questioned the role of the United States in the war found themselves ostracized. But Jeffers did find fault, and in 1948 his own publisher, Random House, proved to be a censor on behalf of American patriotism and idealism.

It may well be that the tenor of the time demanded a less belligerent and isolationist stance than that of Jeffers; his explicit rejection of America's intentions in war and his announcements of apocalypse angered many people. But whatever the reason, Jeffers encountered tremendous difficulty with the publication of his fourteenth book for Random House, *The Double Axe and Other Poems.*

In the only edition of the book published, Random House disavowed Jeffers' ideas with this note following his preface:[1]

The Double Axe and Other Poems is the fourteenth book of verse by Robinson Jeffers published under the Random House imprint. During an association of fifteen years, marked by mutual confidence and accord, the issuance of each new volume has added strength to the close relationship of author and publisher. In all fairness to that constantly interdependent relationship and in complete candor, Random House feels compelled to go on record with its disagreement over some of the political views pronounced by the poet in this volume. Acutely aware of the writer's freedom to express his convictions boldly and forthrightly and of the publisher's function to obtain for him the widest possible hearing, whether there is agreement in principle and detail or not, it is of the utmost importance that difference of views should be wide open on both sides. Time alone is the court of last resort in the case of ideas on trial.

Reviewers of *The Double Axe* quickly recognized the inconsistency of the publisher's disclaimer. In the New York *Herald Tribune,* Ruth Lechlitner noted that [2]

Random House, although the personal beliefs of its editors probably do not coincide with these views of Jeffers—has never felt any need, up to now, to make public statements saying so. Nor do the publishers, apparently feel impelled to repudiate his "philosophical" credo in *The Double Axe.*

The innuendo of this critic's statement, that Jeffers' philosophical credo might have shown cause to be questioned, demonstrates precisely the attitude that the poet came up against in his public. Curiously, this reviewer would allow freedom of political opinion yet the review itself showed little tolerance for Jeffers' doctrine.

The little quarrel of prefaces, from Jeffers' point of view, exemplified one of war's more pernicious effects — the habit of censorship on nationalistic grounds. But the influence on *The Double Axe* of Random House and in particular Jeffers' friend Saxe Commins, a Random House editor, was greater than the prefatory disclaimer might have indicated, for the book, as Jeffers originally envisioned it, was altered considerably. Not only were several poems in *The Double Axe* significantly changed from their original form, but the published volume itself did not contain ten poems that Jeffers intended for publication.

In his preface to the book, Jeffers admitted the impact World War II had upon the text.[3] "But," he wrote, "the poem is not primarily concerned with that grim folly. Its burden . . . is to present a certain philosophical attitude." So the publisher's disclaimer and Commin's editorial advice had nothing to do with the point that Jeffers sought to address. The involvement and the responsibility of the United States in World War II were irrelevant. These matters "are not particularly important," Jeffers wrote, "so far as this book is concerned; they are only the background, or moral climate, of its thought and action."[4] Jeffers' preface clearly indicated that the war was an analogy for certain ideas imbedded in his philosophy, and this, in part, accounted for his use of contemporary figures as metaphors.

The relationship between Jeffers and his publisher was long in developing to the point of open controversy. As early as November 24, 1934, Bennett Cerf, president of Random House, had written to Jeffers, by way of the poet's wife, Una,[5] that Random House had "been doing some quiet campaigning along Pulitzer Prize lines . . . although from the reactions . . .

[he was] afraid that Robin's themes [were] much too strong
and bold to suit the moth-eaten tastes of the doddering old
chaps who award[ed] the Pulitzer Prize."[6] This observation
suggested that Cerf, taking the pulse of the times, felt a duty
to prepare his friend and writer for the impending reaction of
at least some influential people to a poetry as harsh in its view
and as politically frank as that of Jeffers.

In a letter dated April 21, 1938, Cerf wrote that under
separate cover he was sending Jeffers a set of the Roosevelt
papers as a gift to the entire Jeffers family. The volumes were,
in effect, a history of the United States for the Roosevelt years,
and Cerf hoped that Jeffers would want to have them in his
permanent library.[7] This coincidental effort on the part of the
publisher to acknowledge his relationship with the poet was
honest enough (unless it was done to soften the poet's view of
F.D.R.), but for some reason, Cerf either consciously or
unconsciously felt it would be wise to inform his most
holocaustic writer of the achievements of the Roosevelt years
to that date. With war threatening Europe, the United States
was disposed to cast a jaundiced eye toward international
affairs, and as a concerned publisher who knew of Jeffers'
distaste for political machinations, Cerf simply may have
wished to expand the poet's seemingly naive political beliefs.
Although Jeffers acknowledged receiving the generous gift,
there is no indication that he was influenced by the Roosevelt
history.

The same year he gave Jeffers the Roosevelt papers, Cerf
revealed his political ideas to Jeffers in another way. While
vacationing in Europe, he described in a letter to the poet an
air bombardment that he had experienced in Barcelona.[8]

I was scared to death at first but soon got more or less used
to it. After the despair of London and Paris I can't tell you
how really exciting it was to be in a place where the people

are actually fighting to the death for everything in the world that seems most important to me. If the American government allows these wonderful people to be sold out by Chamberlain and his gang, we will have a lot to answer for.

Cerf, then, made his political bent clear to Jeffers. Using "we" for America, the concerned and morally conscious publisher drove home his "country-united" theme. If Bennett Cerf sought to influence Robinson Jeffers during the early and middle years of their association, one must trust that his efforts were unsuccessful and that the poet's verse was published without significant change. Yet, when the manuscript of *The Double Axe* arrived at Random House, there was a peculiar reaction.

In the late forties Robinson Jeffers was a name still respected in literary circles; the publication of a Jeffers book was a special event. The editorial staff had anticipated the arrival of the text of *The Double Axe and Other Poems* months before its actual delivery. But in acknowledging receipt of the manuscript, Saxe Commins wrote:[9]

OCTOBER 15, 1947

MR. ROBINSON JEFFERS
TOR HOUSE
ROUTE 1, BOX 36
CARMEL, CALIFORNIA

DEAR ROBIN:

DURING ALL THESE YEARS, AND IT IS NOW OVER TWENTY, I'VE BEEN WRITING TO UNA, KNOWING OF COURSE YOU WOULD REALIZE THAT MY LETTERS WERE MEANT EQUALLY FOR YOU. ALWAYS I MUST HAVE MADE IT PLAIN HOW MEANINGFUL AND IMPORTANT

EVERY WORD YOU WROTE HAS BEEN TO ME. EVER SINCE ROAN
STALLION, AND IN BOOK AFTER BOOK IN WHICH I WAS SO HONORED
TO HAVE A HAND, MINE WAS A LABOR OF LOVE. AND NOW BEFORE
ANYONE ELSE HAS HAD A CHANCE TO SEE THE MANUSCRIPT OF
THE DOUBLE AXE I MADE A LUNGE FOR IT AS A MATTER OF
EARNED RIGHT. ONCE AGAIN, I WAS MADE TO FEEL YOUR
ELEMENTAL FORCE AND COULD ONLY WONDER AT YOUR ENDLESS
RESOURCES IN CREATING IMAGES AND SYMBOLS OF OVERWHELMING
POWER. HOULT [GORE], AS A SPOKESMAN OF THE YOUNG DEAD IN
WAR, IS INDEED A DARING AND FRIGHTENING CONCEPTION AND HIS
BRUTALITY GROWS OUT OF THE BRUTALITY IN WHICH HE WAS
NURTURED.

BUT I AM DISTURBED AND TERRIBLY WORRIED AND THAT'S WHY I
CAN DO NO LESS THAN BE COMPLETELY CANDID ABOUT MY
MISGIVINGS. I WANT TO PUT THEM DOWN HERE WITHOUT EVEN
MENTIONING THE MATTER TO BENNETT OR ANYONE ELSE AND I
DO SO ENTIRELY ON MY OWN RESPONSIBILITY. I'M COUNTING ON
YOU TO UNDERSTAND MY MOTIVES. I REFER, OF COURSE, TO THE
FREQUENT DAMNING REFERENCES TO PRESIDENT ROOSEVELT.
MANIFESTLY, HE CANNOT DEFEND HIMSELF AND ON THAT SCORE
THERE ARISES THE QUESTION OF FAIRNESS AND GOOD TASTE. BUT
WHAT IS WORSE, IN MY OPINION, IS THE CONVICTION THAT THESE
BITTER CHARGES WILL FEED THE PREJUDICES OF THE WRONG
PEOPLE, ESPECIALLY THOSE WITH THE WORST MOTIVES IN THE
WORLD WHO HAVE TRIED SO HARD AND SO VINDICTIVELY TO
DISCREDIT HIM. IT IS STARTLING INDEED TO FIND THAT TIME
AFTER TIME YOU LASH OUT AT HIS MEMORY AS IF THE NEED TO DO
SO HAS BECOME ALMOST OBSESSIVE: ON PAGE 26 INDIRECTLY, ON
PAGE 29, "TO FEED THE VANITY OF A PARALYTIC," ON PAGES 91,
122, 125, 126, 129, 135, 136, 137[10] (AND HERE FOR THE SECOND
TIME YOU USE THE PHRASE "THE CRIPPLE'S VANITY OF ROOSE-
VELT") AND SO ON, PAGE AFTER PAGE, TO THE END. FRANKLY, I

CANNOT MAKE MYSELF UNDERSTAND IT. THIS MAY BE BECAUSE I DO NOT SHARE YOUR BITTERNESS TOWARDS ROOSEVELT OR HIS HISTORIC ROLE, NOR DO I BELIEVE, AS YOU REITERATE SO FREQUENTLY, THAT THE COUNTRY WAS DRAWN INTO THE CARNAGE BY FOOLS AND TREACHEROUS MEN OR THAT A BETTER DESTINY WOULD AWAIT US IF WE HAD ISOLATED OURSELVES FROM THE REST OF THE WORLD.

AS I SAID, I AM WRITING THIS LETTER ON MY OWN RESPONSIBILITY AND WITH THE HOPE THAT FOR THE SAKE OF YOUR BOOK AND THE EFFECT IT WILL HAVE THAT YOU CAN TEMPER THESE REFERENCES BEFORE WE THINK OF BEGINNING COMPOSITION.

PLEASE UNDERSTAND THAT THIS IS IN NO WAY, AND I CAN'T MAKE THIS TOO EMPHATIC, AN ATTEMPT TO INTRUDE UPON YOUR RIGHTS AS A FREE ARTIST. IT IS MEANT TO BE THE FRIENDLIEST OF SUGGESTIONS MADE WITH THE HOPE THAT YOU CAN BE PERSUADED TO MY STRONGLY PERSONAL VIEWS. I WOULD HATE, ABOVE EVERYTHING ELSE, TO HAVE YOU OF ALL PEOPLE TO BE LINKED WITH REACTIONARY ELEMENTS IN AMERICA. THAT WOULD BE UNTHINKABLE. PLEASE GIVE THIS YOUR MOST SERIOUS THOUGHT AND WRITE TO ME PRIVATELY ABOUT YOUR OWN FEELINGS AS YOU WOULD TO AN OLD FRIEND.

ALWAYS,
SAXE

Jeffers apparently did not reply immediately to his personal plea, which prompted another letter from Commins dated December 4, 1947, reminding the poet that the Random House spring catalog was being prepared and that the revised manuscript of *The Double Axe* was needed for planning purposes.[11] When the revised text did arrive, Commins wrote:[12]

41

IN THIS WILD WATER

FEBRUARY 12, 1948

ROBINSON JEFFERS
TOR HOUSE
ROUTE 1, BOX 36
CARMEL, CALIFORNIA

DEAR ROBIN,

AT LONG LAST I HAVE BEEN ABLE TO GO OVER THE SCRIPT OF The Double Axe. I NOTICED, OF COURSE, ALL THE CHANGES YOU HAVE MADE AND IN ALMOST EVERY INSTANCE THEY ARE IMMENSE IMPROVEMENTS. THERE ARE TWO, HOWEVER, WHICH GIVE RISE TO MISGIVINGS ON MY PART. I REFER TO PAGE TWENTY-FIVE WHERE YOU CHANGE THE LINE "TO FEED THE VANITY OF A PARALYTIC AND MAKE TRICK FORTUNES" TO "TO FEED THE POWER HUNGER OF A PARALYZED MAN AND MAKE TRICK FORTUNES." THIS IS HARDLY A CHANGE AT ALL. WOULD YOU CONSENT TO A REVISION TO MAKE IT READ "TO FEED THE POWER HUNGRY AND MAKE TRICK FORTUNES?" I DO WISH I COULD PERSUADE YOU TO TAKE OUT THE WORD "LITTLE" DESCRIBING TRUMAN ON PAGE 136. TO ME IT SEEMS THE ADJECTIVE REFERRING TO SIZE IS AS GRATUITOUS AN INSULT AS IF YOU DESCRIBED A MAN BY PHYSICAL DEFECT AS "CONSIDER HUNCHBACK STEINMETZ." IT WOULD BE HITTING BELOW THE BELT IN THAT INSTANCE. AS IT IS, YOUR POEM, WITHOUT THE ADJECTIVE, IS CONTEMPTUOUS ENOUGH.

OTHERWISE, I CAN MAKE NO SPECIFIC RECOMMENDATIONS FOR THE CHANGES ALTHOUGH, IN GENERAL, I STILL DISAGREE, AND VEHEMENTLY, WITH SOME OF YOUR INTERPRETATIONS OF RECENT WORLD AND POLITICAL EVENTS AND THE CAUSES UNDERLYING THEM. BUT THAT IS A MATTER OF OPINION AND CONSEQUENTLY OPEN TO DEBATE. CERTAINLY, I CAN'T SUBSCRIBE TO YOUR APOLOGIA FOR PERON WHEN YOU SAY ON PAGE 132 "I WOULD PRAISE ALSO ARGENTINA FOR BEING TOO PROUD TO BAY WITH THE

PACK," NOR YOUR DEFENSE OF ISOLATIONISM IN "HISTORICAL CHOICE," AND IN "FOURTH ACT." I CANNOT SUBSCRIBE TO THE MILDNESS WITH WHICH YOU CHASTEN HITLER, P. 101, AND SCOURGING WITH WHICH YOU FLAY ENGLAND AND AMERICA AND THEIR WAR LEADERS. BECAUSE THESE ARE MATTERS OF OPINION AND YOU HOLD YOURS SO FIRMLY THERE IS A MORAL OBLIGATION TO PRESENT THEM IN YOUR TERMS AND ON YOUR RESPONSIBILITY. BUT LEST THERE BE A MISAPPREHENSION ABOUT THE DIFFERENCE OF VIEWS BETWEEN US, IT OCCURRED TO ME TO WRITE A PUBLISHER'S NOTE ON THE FLAP OF THE JACKET AND ALSO ON THE FRONT OF THE BOOK AS A STATEMENT OF OUR POSITION. HERE IT IS AS I HAVE WRITTEN IT FOR THAT PURPOSE. TELL ME CANDIDLY HOW YOU FEEL ABOUT IT. AT BEST IT IS AN HONEST STATEMENT OF MY VIEWPONT AND AT WORST IT WILL SERVE TO UNDERLINE CERTAIN PASSAGES[13] WHICH OTHERWISE MIGHT EVEN GO UNNOTICED. SINCE BOTH OF US ARE RESPONSIBLE FOR OUR CONVICTIONS AND WE MUST STAND BY THEM, WHY NOT HAVE THEM OUT IN THE OPEN? (PUBLISHER'S DISCLAIMER FOLLOWS.)

To this letter from his editor, Jeffers responded:[14]

TOR HOUSE   CARMEL, CALIFORNIA
RT. 1   BOX 36

FEBRUARY 19, '48.

DEAR SAXE:

(1) IF YOU INSIST, LET THE VERSE READ "TO FEED THE POWER-HUNGER OF A POLITICIAN"—INSTEAD OF "PARALYZED MAN." AND I HOPE YOU WILL ALWAYS PROTEST WHEN CAESAR'S EPILEPSY IS MENTIONED. OR DOSTOEVSKI'S THOUGH IT INFLUENCED HIS GENIUS, JUST AS ROOSEVELT'S PARALYSIS INFLUENCED, AND TO SOME EXTENT EXCUSES, HIS CHARACTER. THIS WAS MY REASON FOR SPEAKING OF IT.

(2) As to "little Truman"—the adjective cannot possibly refer to physical size, since Truman is a bigger man than either Churchill (except the fat) or Hitler. But you will admit that he is "little" in a historical sense (and also "innocent") compared to either of them. However—to show you what a good fellow I am—Write "Harry," if it really matters to you, instead of "little."

(3) As to other things, I'm sorry we don't agree completely. And I do agree that Hitler deserves worse than he gets but you know the whole world is full of people cursing Hitler.

(4) As to the suggested "Publisher's Note"—it will certainly make every reader think of politics rather than poetry, and is therefore deplorable. But put it in, by all means, if it is a matter of conscience. I shall probably in that case have to add a short paragraph to my own "Note," saying that any political judgments in the book are not primary but part of the background, the moral climate of the time as I see it; and perhaps ending with a sentence from Shaw's preface to "Heartbreak House"—I quote badly, from memory—"Only a man who has lived attentively through a general war, not as a member of the military, but as a civilian, *and kept his head,* can understand the bitterness. . . . "

(5) No—I don't think of any dedication.

Thanks for your clear and fair letter. And for your not complaining about the dirty manuscript—I didn't have time or energy to type it over again. It was a joy to see you recently; and I hope to repeat the pleasure if we go to Ireland this spring, as appears likely.

Yours—
Robinson Jeffers

These letters point to a delicate area in the relationship between editor and author, for it was in the substance of the excised poems that the contention lay.

Within the omitted poems — "Miching Mallecho," "Fantasy," "The Blood Guilt," "Wilson in Hell," "What Odd Expedients," "Ordinary Newscaster," "Staggering Back Toward Life," "Curb Science," "War Guilt Crimes," and "Pourvou Que Ca Doure," — Jeffers defined his doctrine of inhumanism more clearly and applied it more broadly; the poems also revealed the intensity of Jeffers' conviction and the extent to which he carried the doctrine. The correspondence between Commins and the poet concerning the relative appropriateness of the verses and Commins' plea to moderate the tone of those verses, reveals little about whether the poems would have been published had Jeffers refused to alter some poems and to delete others. The expunged poems emphasized and colored what has been so frequently misunderstood by Jeffers' readers: that inhumanism was an attitude, a means to an end; it was not an ultimatum.

It is important to remember that Jeffers' inhumanism was a rigorous and demanding doctrine. Observing and interpreting nature, he took a lesson from the nonhuman: survival was a gift to the fittest, who demanded and should receive no quarter in what was always a fight for survival. Jeffers saw himself as fighting for the life of each element of the universe and for the integrity of the whole.

In his first response to *The Double Axe,* Saxe Commins drew upon his personal friendship with Jeffers to plead for moderation and good taste. His second letter established a rationale for the publisher's note. The complete motive behind Commins' disclaimer may never be known, but the private friend became the public editor, speaking of "our position" (presumably, that of Random House).

Apparently without reading the manuscript, Bennett Cerf also had celebrated its arrival:[15]

OCTOBER 7, 1947

DEAR UNA:

THE MANUSCRIPT OF ROBIN'S NEW BOOK, THE DOUBLE AXE, ARRIVED THIS AFTERNOON AND ELICITED CHEERS FROM THE ENTIRE EDITORIAL DEPARTMENT.

AS EVER,
BENNETT

This was one week before Commins made his first response. Eventually, however, Cerf read the manuscript and agreed with Commins' position, as his letter to Una on March 18, 1948, indicated.[16]

MEANWHILE, I HOPE YOU ARE PLEASED WITH THE WAY ROBIN'S NEW BOOK IS GOING TO BE PRESENTED TO THE PUBLIC. MY OWN OPINION IS THAT THE SLIGHTLY CONTROVERSIAL FOOTNOTE ABOUT OUR RESPECTIVE IDEOLOGIES HAS BEEN PHRASED PERFECTLY BY SAXE COMMINS AND MOST CERTAINLY WILL ATTRACT ADDED SPACE AND ATTENTION FROM THE REVIEWERS.

AS EVER,
BENNETT

Clearly, both men spoke for the corporate Random House in emphasizing the disparity between the publisher and the poet and in sheltering their dissent in a corporate identity. At this point they removed themselves from the role that they were to play as publisher to a role that permitted them to use their author's art, in effect, as a vehicle to voice their own philosophy.

If Jeffers was discouraged and inhibited by his publisher's objections to some of the more pointed ramifications of his philosophy of inhumanism, one can well imagine his reaction to the even harsher treatment he received in some of the reviews of *The Double Axe*. Dudley Fitts, writing in the *New York Times Book Review,* spoke of "the violent Mr. Jeffers." Fitts claimed that *The Double Axe* "opens beautifully but after the first page the moments of conviction, of poetical (or, for that matter, moral) validity are decreasingly frequent."[17] Jeffers' "agonist . . . mouth[s] hysterical extremely shopworn patchenisms[18] on the subject of war," Fitts wrote. Pointing up this latter phenomenon, the reviewer quoted:

> *You'll be there, old man, right*
> *   along with the president*
> *And his paid mouths; and the*
> *   radio shouters, the writers,*
> *   the world-planners, the heavy*
> *   bishops,*
> *The England-lovers, the little*
> *   poets and college professors.*
> *Swing high, swing low. . . .*

The irony was, of course, that Jeffers numbered himself among "the England-lovers, the little / poets." But Fitts went on to comment:

True, these are the sentiments of young Hoult Gore; but there is evidence in short lyrics printed in this book that they are not repugnant to Mr. Jeffers, and it is significant that Random House, in an extraordinary prefatory statement, disclaims any share in them. Their depressing quality is not so much a high-school morality as a high-school cheapness; which is, after all, only another aspect of Mr. Jeffers' violence.

Curiously, the reviewer acknowledged the "extraordinary prefatory statement" by the publisher yet did not address the publisher's rationale for its presence. By denying the metaphoric value of the poetry and by comparing Jeffers with his protagonist, Hoult Gore, Fitts contentedly left the reader to assume that the disclaimer was appropriate.

Time magazine discussed the disclaimer in a prepublication comment entitled "Chapter and Verse." *Time* saw the need for a disclaimer as an antidote to Jeffers' special power:[19]

> The persuasive powers of poetry got thumping recognition from Robinson Jeffers' publisher. Next month Jeffers' new book of verse would [*sic*] contain a cautious note-to-the-reader: "Random House feels compelled to go on record with its disagreement over some of the political views pronounced by the poet in this volume. . . . "

Several issues later a review in *Time,* under the caption "And Buckets O'Blood," noted that "readers of this book of poems are advised in a highly unusual (and ungrammatical) publisher's note that Random House does not agree with some of the political views pronounced by the poet Robinson Jeffers."[20] Suspicions about the disclaimer, however, did not keep the anonymous reviewer from disparaging the volume:[21]

> Jeffers' political views are, in fact, stark and skinny as a buzzard's craw.

Gerald McDonald, chief of the American History Division of the New York Public Library, claimed that Jeffers' "violent, hateful book [was] a gospel of isolationism carried beyond geography, faith and hope. Civilization is an evil, war and peace are equally evil, Christianity and communism, leaders and little men are all contemptible."[22]

48

Review upon review noted the violence, and some reviewers suspected that the poet would deny the survival of "human kindness or decency."[23] Yet, as aggressive as the commentaries were, they shared one underlying assumption: that the poet must be allowed his say.

The reviews do, however, point up one peculiarity: whatever their reaction to Jeffers' verse, the reviewers acknowledged the publisher's note but did not inquire about its genesis. Because of the uniqueness of the disclaimer, the reviewers should have recognized that there must have been at least some discussion between poet and publisher before such a note was published. Unfortunately, the lack of investigation can be easily accounted for as another indication of the times. Safeguarding national policy from verse bearing little good will was accepted without question. Jeffers' readers had aesthetic, philosophical, and psychological interests in his poems; but the reviewers had an obligation to do more than accept the disclaimer at face value.

Knowing that Jeffers' original manuscript for *The Double Axe* was in part changed to conform with the wishes of Random House, one can better understand the "trans-human magnificence" to which Jeffers subscribed and that made him seem to many reviewers, let alone his publisher, a violent and immoral man. The poet's belief that only by rejecting solipsism could man peacefully gain his place in the universe is no better illustrated than by his acquiescence in the face of his publisher's unsympathetic and often bitter reaction to his verse. Rather than compromise his philosophy, Jeffers subscribed to it functionally by yielding to editorial opinion. Despite his acquiescence, however, Jeffers was motivated to respond to the decision of Random House to include a disclaimer.

He wrote:[24]

MARCH 2, '48

DEAR SAXE:

WILL YOU PLEASE SUBSTITUTE THE ENCLOSED PAGE FOR THE "NOTE" THAT I THINK IS PAGE (1) OF THE MANUSCRIPT?
—AS YOU SEE, IT IS PRACTICALLY THE SAME THING, EXCEPT ONE PARAGRAPH ADDED IN RESPONSE TO YOUR "PUBLISHER'S NOTE." AND SINCE THERE ARE NOW THREE PARAGRAPHS I CALL IT "PREFACE!"

BEST WISHES—
ROBIN

To which Commins responded:[25]

MARCH 4, 1948

MR. ROBINSON JEFFERS
TOR HOUSE
CARMEL-BY-THE-SEA, CALIF.

DEAR ROBIN:

MANY THANKS FOR SENDING ME THE NEW PREFACE. HERE IS THE OLD ONE. I AM REALLY HAPPY THAT YOU HAVE STATED YOUR POSITION SO CLEARLY AND PRECISELY. EVEN THOUGH WE DIFFER, IT IS CERTAINLY REASONABLE THAT OUR OPINIONS SHOULD BE STATED FORTHRIGHTLY. IT WILL BE INTERESTING TO WATCH THE REACTION OF A JURY OF READERS.

BEST TO YOU AND UNA.

YOURS,
SAXE COMMINS

Apparently Random House was not fully prepared to allow for the fallibility or perniciousness of humanity, at least as it was stated in Jeffers' uncompromising terms. Moved by personal and, it is hoped, altruistic motives, the publisher dampened the public's opportunity for introspection. Robert Fitzgerald, in the *New Republic,* saw Jeffers from a typical perspective.[26]

> Robinson Jeffers . . . has cast a cold eye on life and death and in his best fragments has written lines, rather hugely and coldly hewn, that truthfully honor the life of rock-faces and external nature; but on a review of his work these out-croppings sink into a quagmire of appalling primitivism from which not even a pterodactyl could take wing. He has been trying to say to all men: "You are corrupted monsters, unworthy of a single mountain range," and in *The Double Axe* he outdoes himself in the violence of the saying; the two long fables of the volume are full of blood and carrion and incestuous horror. . . . The trouble is not in the poet's initial emotion; it is in the mindlessness of its working out; the sheer bombast and fantasy of it, like the vileness that small boys make up to turn each other's stomachs.

The "appalling primitivism" to which Fitzgerald objected was the condition of humanity that Jeffers saw. Given his philosophical stance, Jeffers would brook little of man's anthropocentricity. His method, in a world of struggle, was to grasp the throats of his race—to catch them breathless.

Reviewing *The Double Axe* in the *Saturday Review of Literature,* Seldon Rodman, who regarded Jeffers as "perhaps our foremost poet," worried that Jeffers may have become "totally irresponsible, politically, poetically, humanly," in his assumption that "Germany could have been permitted to impose slavery on the rest of the world, that our leaders spoke only for themselves and from the vilest of motives, and that from now on we have nothing better to do than to give our hearts to the hawks." Rodman, representative of many of Jeffers' readers, was unaware of the final import of the publisher's note that preceded the poems. Noting that *The Double Axe* was "spiked . . . with a belligerently 'isolationist' preface by the author," he took Jeffers' political view at face value. But, he commented further,[27]

> Random House deserves credit for publishing this book. Jeffers, whatever one may think of his philosophy, remains as close to a major poet as we have. We have much to learn from him. It did not require a play ("Medea," 1946) to establish his preeminence in dramatics. The first part of the title poem in "The Double Axe" is as gripping and power-fully paced as any of his early narratives. In the shorter pieces he retains that ability, shown sporadically by Mac-Leish and Sandburg in the Thirties and then abandoned by them, to speak straight (and hotly) on "hot" political issues without hedging his meaning in any of the fashionable contortions of symbolic double-talk, and without sacrificing the spare magnificence of his own style. We must respect his integrity . . . [N]uances of tone, ambiguities of meaning, felicities of language and music, are not to be looked for in his verse. . . . It is sad that as the years go by he repeats himself endlessly; that he elects to close his eyes to human heroism and goodness and to manmade beauty; and that he feels compelled to add more than his quota of hatred and violence to the hatred and violence abroad in the world, while he sits in that properly inhuman stone tower of his waiting exultantly for the bomb.

In one voice praising Jeffers, then, Rodman denounced him in another.

But to declare his poetry devoid of ambiguity of meaning and "nuances of tone" would be to deny it as poetry. Exploration of *The Double Axe,* as the book was originally conceived of, shows the converse to be the case; Jeffers' poetry was indeed intense and imaginative, though often an inconsistent rendering of his perceptions of the world, man, and the interrelationship of the two. The very nature of Jeffers' philosophical stance, his verse, its public reception, its critical commentary, points up the need to place Jeffers' inhumanism into a proper perspective.

There is little doubt that the cause of the confusion created by *The Double Axe* was the deletion of the ten poems from its text by publishers hostile to the poet's ideology. A careful look at the poems of *The Double Axe* will bring a better understanding of how Robinson Jeffers' philosophy dictated certain poetic devices and characteristics that were repugnant to his publishers and to most reviewers.

4.

THE STONES OF WHITENESS

In the ten excised poems, one can recognize many of the themes present in *The Double Axe and Other Poems*. Their controlling concern is the inhumanist's intense pronouncement for the future. Jeffers spoke against patriotism and chastised Hitler, Churchill, and Truman. He questioned the demagogues and world-redeemers who, in his words, had "duped us" with lies and malice. "Man has been queer from the start," Jeffers wrote; "civilization is sick." Acknowledging that his intention as an author was to disgust and shock his readers, Jeffers said that monsters possessed the world. He used animal metaphors and similes to place man in a context that partially denied what Jeffers believed to be a fatal anthropocentricity. What Jeffers sought to spell out was the cause-and-effect relationship between man's present and complex circumstances and the future. In *The Double Axe* Jeffers pondered over the nature of man's existence. The poet preached an "aesthetic emotion" because to the inhumanist "all existed for beauty," and not for human advancement, security, or happiness.[1]

> *Certainly the world*
> *Was not constructed for happiness nor love nor wisdom.*
> *No, nor for pain, hatred and folly. All these*
> *Have their seasons; and in the long year they balance*
> *Each other, they cancel out. But the beauty stands*

The respective tables of contents, juxtaposed on the next page, suggest some of the alterations (italics denotes a modified poem, bold face denotes an expunged poem).

"Aesthetic emotion" allowed for the inconsequentiality of the human effort. There would be war in the human future just as there had been war in the past; the impending decay of Europe was emblematic of the decay of civilization. Essentially, then, Jeffers was asking man to be cognizant of beauty because, abstract as it is, beauty symbolized the changelessness that inhumanism would have man recognize and admire.

Another theme found throughout *The Double Axe* and especially in the excised poems related to the future, specifically, the idea that "fate has man in hand" and man's role is merely to exist. It was to be hoped that man would do so in harmony with other things in the universe. Jeffers' cynicism was nowhere as strong as it was in the excised poems that dealt with this naturalistic fatalism, where he admitted that his philosophy was "bitter counsel but necessary."

The relative worth of the poems that Saxe Commins and Bennett Cerf excised from the manuscript may be determined only by a close examination of their artistic accomplishments and validity. Are they poems that merely serve a political vendetta, or do they enlarge, deepen, and validate Robinson Jeffers' philosophic and artistic concerns? Variation in the quality of the excised work is immediately apparent. Some of the poems are complex and carefully composed; others are

merely interesting; a few are inadequate. But all radiate aspects of Jeffers' stark philosophy of inhumanism. Although the excised poems may attack political systems and criticize personalities, they are logical extensions of Jeffers' thought and, as such, they must be considered seriously.

In the poem "Miching Mallecho" Jeffers speaks of youth and old age. Although the subject of their relationship is unique to the excised poems, Part I of "The Double Axe," "The Love and the Hate," involves a son's hate for what his father sanctions.[2] Hoult Gore, killed on a Pacific island, returns to torment his parents for being

> *the decent and loyal people of America,*
> *Caught by their own loyalty, fouled, gouged and bled*
> *To feed the power-hunger of the politicians and make trick*
> > *fortunes*
> *For swindlers and collaborators.*

Hoult demands that his father "tell [him] one decent reason / why the United States got into" the war, and later he shoots him, saying:

> > *"Poor old worm, the race*
> > > *is fixed.*
> *You cannot win it. I don't hate him at all, it's justice.*
> *I wish that every man who approved this war,*
> > *In which we had no right, reason nor justice,*
> > *Were crawling there. . . . "*

In the fire that consumes his father, Hoult sees the faces of "Tojo," "Roosevelt," a "Captain Blasted" who had been shot in the back, his father "Bull Gore, bellowing," and "Davy Larson," his mother's lover.

Miching Mallecho
(*May 1941*)

Wagging their hoary heads, glaring through their bright
*   spectacles,*
The old gentlemen shout for war, while youth,
Amazed, unwilling, submissive, watches them. This is not normal,
But really ominous. It is good comedy,
But for a coming time it means mischief. The boys have memories.

In "Miching Mallecho" Jeffers actually warns of the future: in discussing the relationship between "old gentlemen" and "youth" he cautions: "But for a coming time it means mischief. The boys have memories." He forecasts trouble by suggesting that these "boys" who are now "submissive" will someday retaliate. This warning also reveals the perception and sensitivity of the inhumanist speaker. Jeffers' stance betrays a certain amount of altruism by implicitly hoping for the remote future while condemning the present and claiming "mischief" for a future time. In context, "mischief" appears to be an understatement: youth is persuaded to war—a rather tragic occurrence ominous of more bloodshed. To the inhumanist, the victimization of "youth" is not normal; "the boys have memories."

The inhumanist feels the uncertainty of the future. "Youth" may assume the role of those "old gentlemen" and themselves someday promote war; or, "youth" may assume a reactionary stance, and—in effect—war with their elders here and now. Here is the double axe; it cuts both ways.

In the teaching relationship between youth and "old gentlemen" (the Establishment?), Jeffers finds an abnormality; he finds cause for cynicism pronounced elsewhere. It was during the spring of 1941, a time when the United States was carefully watching the Axis powers metastasize Europe, that Jeffers wrote of the "old gentlemen" and their shouts for war. He gives us an image of worthy and wise old men, passing fervent judgment on what they see through "bright spectacles." The youth of the nation watch the elders skeptically. "This is not normal," the poet warns, "but really ominous." Jeffers worries about the unconscionable influence that the nationalistic "old gentlemen" have upon the "youth"; yet he sees this situation satirically as "good comedy." The poet insinuates a certain amount of naiveté, as well as "sneaking mischief" on the part of the old gentlemen who deceive the youth. This is the same naiveté that allowed[3]

> *the President*
> *And his paid mouths; and the radio-shouters, the writers,*
> *the world-planners, the heavy bishops,*
> *The England-lovers, the little poets and college*
> *professors,*
> *The seducers of boys, the pimps of death,*

to dupe the "old gentlemen" even as they would, perhaps innocently, dupe the "youth." This is a relationship of polarities that is caused by what Jeffers calls a "bitter need" to deceive.

Jeffers took his title for "Miching Mallecho" from *Hamlet*. The expression comes from lines occurring after the dumb show, "The Murder of Gonzago," which Hamlet had planned to expose Claudius as the deceitful slayer of his father. When the show ends, Ophelia asks, "What means this my Lord?" to which Hamlet replies, "Marry, this is miching mallecho; it means mischief." More precisely, it means "sneaking mischief."[4] The clever use of the Spanish words suggest the theme of this poem. "Miching Mallecho" is a trap that dramatizes the insidiousness of men of responsibility who are given over to deceit.

The polarity between youth and age defines the theme. The "old gentlemen" are likened to pets "wagging their hoary heads." The image is strongly evocative and calls to mind doddering old fools who maintain an intellectual posture and who (note the pun on "hoary") prostitute themselves to "shout for war." The inhumanist believes that man, as a part of the universe, ought to live for better purposes and have a more reasoned perspective than to advocate war. Somewhat facetiously, the poet describes the "old gentlemen" as "glaring through their bright spectacles." If the spectacles are eyeglasses through which the vision of the old men is supposed to be made clear, the poet ironically sees no clarity in their vision. Jeffers' use of "bright" shows how the old men see. Their vision is their prognosis for war, another, more deadly kind of "bright spectacle." Caught up in this fervor, they shout.

In youth one proverbially expects the promised hope of the future. In saying that "the boys have memories" Jeffers implies that "youth" will even the score when they are older and have assumed positions of decision. The words "amazed" and "unwilling" lend credence to whatever hope is implied in "youth"; they are not now of the same bent as the "old gentlemen." Curiously, a structural and visual vacillation occurs as the poet moves from the stronger adjectives to "submissive." Jeffers accentuates an ambivalence in "youth" by gently admonishing them as complacent. The verb "watches" plays both on "spectacles," for "youth" would seem to have no artificial visions, and on "while," for youth is a time in which one idly watches the assignation of destiny from the perspective of the inhumanist; youth mimes age as it grows old and supersedes the generation before. Youth is going to fight the war the "old gentlemen" call for. Hence, the "mischief" of the old men.

An Ordinary Newscaster
(*January 13, '44*)

I heard a radio-parrot, an ordinary newscaster
Say this: "Tonight the German astronomers
Will be looking up at the sky: the moon will eclipse the planet Jupiter:
    if our bombers come over
They'll look again." He said with the pride of patriotism, "The
    German astronomers
Are interested in the red spot on Jupiter, they hope the eclipse will
    help them learn something more
About the red spot. But Our brave kids are interested only in the
    red flashes.
Made by their falling bombs."
                This is perhaps the most ignoble statement
    we have heard yet, but unfortunately
It is in the vein. We are not an ignoble people; rather
    generous; but having been tricked
A step at a time, cajoled, scared, smacked with war, a decent
    inexpert people, betrayed by men
Whom it thought it could trust: our whole attitude
Stinks of that ditch. So will the future peace.

"An Ordinary Newscaster" casts a cause-and-effect relationship between *The Double Axe* theme of deceptive leaders and a future destined to trouble. The American has "been tricked" into war, betrayed by his leaders, duped into abandoning the detached and knowledge-seeking position that apparently characterizes the German astronomers. And if the present "stinks of that ditch," "so will the future peace." The inhumanist worries that the future will be colored by the meanness and excessive fervor that is typified by the broadcaster.

The American people have lost their sense of relationship to the cosmos. They no longer develop a perspective by studying nature; they are preoccupied with a provisional patriotism and the dropping of bombs. The poet illustrates this concern in the parable of the newscaster. Jeffers contrasts what appears to be the German's interest in scientific truth with the American's obsession with jingoism and revenge—a theme taken up in "War-Guilt Trials." The "ordinary newscaster" gloats over the prospect of American planes interrupting the German astronomers who would be looking up at Jupiter. The Germans, Jeffers relates, are interested in the red spot on Jupiter—made more available on this particular night to telescopic scrutiny because of the eclipse; the Americans, more mundanely, are interested in the red spots of war. That the newscaster is "ordinary," or typical, manifests Jeffers' thoughts about what has happened to the American people because of the war. "Not an ignoble people" by nature (indeed, actually a "generous" people), the Americans have shrunk to a meanness in which they are obsessed with matters of patriotism and passion rather than science and truth.

Seldom is the poet's partisanship so vigorous as in this poem; seldom is his hypothesis so blatant. But the emphasis should be noted: it is not a poem arguing the German cause. Jeffers is aligning himself more with the *scientist* (who happens to be German, than with the *patriot* (who happens to be American.) And Jeffers takes this position because of his inhumanism, which urges the exploration, purely scientific or otherwise, of truth.

"Fantasy" demonstrates that Jeffers' inhumanism gave him no immediate hope for man's ability to achieve a lasting peace. The reader is well aware of the cyclic theory of history and of alternations in the state of the world; once at war, then at peace. Yet man's nature remains the same. He is an animal with an irreversible impulse to conflict. The end of a war brings new hope to man, and "Fantasy" considers this possibility for the reader. Then, without forewarning, that pleasant interlude is dealt a disquieting blow.

Fantasy
(Written in June 1941)

Finally in white innocence
The fighter planes like swallows dance,
The bombers above ruined towns
Will drop wreaths of roses down,
Doves will nest in the guns' throats
And the people dance in the streets,
Whistles will bawl and bells will clang,
On that great day the boys will hang
Hitler and Roosevelt in one tree,
Painlessly, in effigy,
To take their rank in history;
Roosevelt, Hitler and Guy Fawkes
Hanged above the garden walks,
While the happy children cheer,
Without hate, without fear,
And new men plot a new war.

The poet would have the reader imagine a time when "bombers . . . will drop wreaths of roses down," when "doves will nest in guns' throats." The joyous dance of peace and innocence has finally begun, "without hate, without fear." Even the potentially sobering act of meting out justice to war criminals is sublimated into the act of hanging them *in effigy*. All feelings and deeds of violence, it would seem, have disappeared; goodness and mercy appear to have inherited the earth.

The neat, crisp rhythm, the simple and perfect rhyme, the monosyllables, the easy syntax, and the plain and familiar images—all reinforce the sense of the honest, innocent, and youthful joy of this fantasy. And then, quite matter-of-factly, comes the jolt: "new men plot a new war." Unseen and unsuspected, men plan new conflicts all over again. This last line, ironically the final statement of the fantasy, destroys the superficial picture of peace and innocence drawn earlier. The emphatic suggestion is that the state of youth, like joy and innocence, is in fact a state of naiveté. By punctuating his poem with this final and unrhymed line, Jeffers points up the vulnerability of the "happy children" who rejoice complacently and unsuspectingly in the peace, and the brutality of those "new men" who "plot a new war."

The inhumanist positions himself as detached observer; he sides with neither the dancers nor the plotters. He can see both with equal clarity, and he makes it all appear somehow inevitable. In a sense, "Fantasy" is a poem more brutal for having seemed at first so pleasant. One might have anticipated this harsh view from Herman Melville or Emily Dickinson, whose antiromantic bitterness Jeffers shared. (Indeed, Jeffers forewarns the reader in "Miching Mallecho" that "the boys have memories"; that very likely they could be their fathers' sons, and move into war as did the "old gentlemen.")

That "Fantasy" is so typical of Jeffers' work in *The Double Axe* is perhaps all the more reason to question the judgment of Random House in asking Jeffers to delete this poem. The publisher's letters to the poet, presented in Chapter 3, may simply indicate disapproval of Jeffers' linking Roosevelt with Hitler and Guy Fawkes.[5] If this is the case, an engaging and well-made poem, set in an American tradition of antiromanticism, has been sacrificed for partisan opinion. This poem, one of the best of those excised, is probably better—in terms of form and effect—than most of the poems left in *The Double Axe.*

67

Staggering Back Toward Life

Radar and rocket-plane, the applications of chemistry, the tricks of
  physics: new cunning rather
Than new science: but they work. The time is in fact
A fever-crisis; the fag-end of nominal peace before these wars, and the
  so-called peace to follow them,
Are, with the wars, one fever; the world one hospital;
The semi-delirious patient his brain breeds dreams like flies, but they
  are giants. And they work. The question is
How much of this amazing lumber the pale convalescent
Staggering back toward life will be able to carry up the steep gorges
  that thrid the cliffs of the future?
I hope, not much. We need a new dark-age, five hundred years of winter
  and the tombs for dwellings—but it's remote still.

In "Staggering Back Toward Life" Jeffers addresses what he takes to be the sickness of civilization and its bearing on the future. Jeffers speaks of the efforts and dreams of man that have brought the world through wars interspersed with nominal peace to a condition of "fever-crisis." Thus he sees that the world is "one hospital." He questions just how much of man's effort and fantasy can be utilized in his attempt to build a future. He hopes "not much," for the building blocks that man seeks to work with are "amazing lumber." Those materials, taking origin from man's present state of delirium, are hardly suitable for bringing him up "the steep gorges that thrid the cliffs of the future." Jeffers' panacea for the "pale convalescent" is a "new dark-age, five hundred years of winter / and the tombs for dwellings." But even after such a washing away of man's disposition for war, the possibility for a viable future is remote. The poet speaks of this burden that man has assumed in foregoing "new science" as "amazing." Because of his inhumanism, Jeffers is bewildered by man's predicament;

consequently, he hopes that the cause of the "fever-crisis" will not hold over and accompany man as he strives toward the future. Even with a "new dark-age" Jeffers is skeptical that man will lose the "amazing lumber" to which he has grown accustomed.

The form and substance of this somewhat prosaic and propagandistic poem serve to point up Jeffers' cynical view of mankind's irregular state of being: man lives under what ultimately may prove to be a burden too difficult for him to bear. In referring to the applications of science as "tricks" and "new cunning," Jeffers thematically links the poem to "Miching Mallecho." The suspicions of the inhumanist cause him naturally to cast a jaundiced eye toward instruments of science that are adapted for war. He sees the applications of chemistry and the tricks of physics as the appendages, so to speak, of those who discover and disguise their use. Sick men do not seek a new understanding by means of science but rather develop a new disguise for old cunning. Jeffers addresses this idea in "An Ordinary Newscaster" as well when he ironically compares the German astronomers — scientists — to the American patriotic "kids," who are too immature and too caught up in nationalism to seek scientific truths.

In "Staggering Back Toward Life" Jeffers finds that the scientific efforts of man are inquiries for deception rather than for knowledge and truth. Nevertheless, these efforts "work." Science, the poet says, is operative no matter what the intentions of man. But the misapplications of science are not "new science" but "new cunning." And when Jeffers says that "the time is in fact / a fever-crisis," he is addressing man's disposition, which leads him to this "new cunning" and away from what should be his search: the objective truths of "new science." He would warn us that the auspices under which chemistry and physics progress are of no importance; the applications of that progress will determine whether or not man pursues truth. Under the conditions in which science is perverted, the world has become "one hospital," and the inhabitant of this world, "the semi-delirious patient his brain breeds dreams like flies." The ambiguity of this simile points up the difficulty of man's predicament: the inhumanist sees a prolific imagination producing desires beyond the capability of achievement; he sees these dreams likened to common and disease-ridden insects. (Note the irony in "flies," meaning also "distractions.") But no matter how much a fantasy the dreams are, no matter how many there are, and no matter how detrimental their application is — the dreams work. They do so much in the same way the "applications of chemistry" and the "tricks of physics" work. They are "amazing lumber." The future is remote.

Another of the excised poems that discusses the theme of man's future is "What Odd Expedients." As in several of *The Double Axe* poems, Jeffers considers God's role in the affairs of man. In making God responsible for man's behavior, Jeffers comments: "God uses strange means for great purposes." In this poem, Jeffers implies a Calvinist theology; all is predetermined by the godhead; man lives to carry out the plan according to destiny. At the crux of the poem are the "odd expedients" that comprise those "strange means" that the poet claims for God. These are the "crackpot dreams of Jeanne d'Arc and Hitler; / the cripple's-power-need of Roosevelt; the bombast / Of Mussolini; the tinsel star of Napoleon; the pitiful idiot / submissiveness / Of peoples to leaders and men to death," all of which promote war. The "great purpose" for which God would further war is achieved by letting man act out his capacities and his energies, but at the same time limiting man's power to affect the universe. One can sense the sarcasm of inhumanism in the irony of this situation: man is a creature, "locally omnipotent," but with energies and desires that make him reach far beyond his ability to implement or

What Odd Expedients

God, whether by unconscious instinct, or waking, or in a dream, I do
    not know how conscious is God,
Uses strange means for great purposes. His problem with the human
    race is to play its capacities
To their extreme limits, but limit its power. For how dull were the
    little planet, how mean and splendorless,
If all one garden; and man locally omnipotent rested the energies that
    only need, only
Bitter need breeds.
        The solution of course is war, which both goads and
    frustrates; and to promote war
What odd expedients! The crackpot dreams of Jeanne d'Arc and Hitler;
    the cripple's-power-need of Roosevelt; the bombast
Of Mussolini; the tinsel star of Napoleon; the pitiful idiot
    submissiveness
Of peoples to leaders and men to death:—what low means toward high
    aims!—the next chapter of the world
Hangs between the foreheads of two strong bulls ranging one field.
    Hi, Red! Hi, Whitey!

control them. Perhaps this is the "bitter need" Jeffers speaks of; having the desire but not the ability to effect it, man turns upon himself, turns to war. Jeffers describes these "odd expedients" as "low means" and therefore beneath the dignity of a God who created man and beneath the dignity of man who is capable of being part of "one garden." Seldom is the inhumanist so sympathetic to man's plight. This poem offers, in effect, an apologia for man's behavior. Yet, an abiding cynicism remains: if God has given man enough rope, man is in the process of hanging himself.

The gratuitous last lines are curious: they are nondramatic, didactic, and presumptuous in pronouncing God's will.

(Peculiarly, *The Double Axe* poem "Teheran" uses the same metaphor, "there will be Russia / and America; two powers alone in the world; two bulls / in one pasture. And what is unlucky Germany / Between those foreheads?" But in "What Odd Expedients," the metaphor is more explicit and guides the reading.) These lines read best as a prophecy of inhumanism addressing the tentativeness of the future. The clever poetics of the lines allow some argument for their presence. Going from "foreheads" to "two bulls" to "one field," Jeffers moves us through a countdown in which a lifetime is ticked off to death. (In a sense, this is the cosmic "oneness" to which inhumanism subscribes.) As humanity "plays its capacities / To their extreme limits," they are reduced to "bulls,"[6] self-appointed policemen of the world—stubborn, awkward, and intrusive. The irony is that they range "one field." These bulls, symbolic of danger, strength, and fertility, cover the universe. Jeffers plays on "one field," which connotes that singular environment conducive to the continuation of all species as well as being a place for fulfillment, a range. But the prognosis is for sterility and conflict. They cannot mate; they can only fight. Their contact "goads and frustrates"; it allows no propagation of the race, perhaps only self-destruction.

In the early forties, Jeffers probably considered the two "bulls" as political ideologies that were to absorb, for the most part, the energies of man. In the traditional vein, these ideologies were given the analogues "red" and "white": "red" for communism and, particularly, Russia; "white" for anti-communism and, particularly, the United States. Undoubtedly the poet appreciated that these ideologies should be called "red" and "white": red symbolized the martyrdom and bloodshed that was to come and white symbolized purity as well as death and decay. For the poet of inhumanism it was the latter implication of whiteness that all men achieve as long as these expedients are the only means by which men can achieve that which is theirs only to attain.

72

Pourvou Que Ca Doure

Life grows, life is not made; you can make death. Neither were the sun
*   nor the stars created,*
But grew from what grew before. Without the corruption of plants and
*   corpses life could not grow.*
Look around you at civilization decaying and sick: look at science,
*   corrupted*
To be death's bawd; and art—painting and sculpture, that had some
*   dignity—*
Corrupted into the show-off antics of an imbecile child; and statecraft
Into the democratic gestures of a gin-muddled butcher-boy: look all
*   around you,*
And praise the solitary hawk-flights of God, and say, what a stinking of
*   famous corpses*
To fertilize the fields of the human future . . . if man's back holds.

Of the excised poems, "Pourvou Que Ca Doure" perhaps
demonstrates a higher degree of poetic merit than most of the
other poems. The poem brings together *The Double Axe*
themes of "civilization decaying and sick," natural evolution,
and a concern for man's future. Translated from the French,
"provided that it lasts," the title refers to the last line of the
poem, "if man's back holds," a line that comments on the
burden of rampant corruption men have to bear if life is to
continue. Jeffers directs us to "look all around" and see that
life grows from death. Things are corrupted: science, art, and
statecraft are "famous corpses" "stinking." Yet everything
comes from what precedes it, and new forms evolve from the
old—but only if man can live.

Jeffers bids us submit to the oneness of nature and the
motion of the universe in the charge: "And praise the solitary
hawk-flights of God." He asks that man acknowledge death,
corruption, and the cause for "civilization decaying and sick."

73

Science, as suggested also in "Staggering Back Toward Life," has been misused for war and other such purposes precipitous of death; art, once of some stature, has been reduced to the "show-off antics of an imbecile child"; and statecraft has been lessened to "democratic gestures of a gin-muddled butcher-boy." Man must bear the weight of this civilization if he is to continue to live.

Jeffers repeats an earlier theme in giving the reader an alternative to self-destruction and an opportunity for a future. This alternative, a tenet of inhumanism, calls for acknowledging the nature of things and the relationship of man to nature: death and decay are building blocks in a natural cycle of life. Jeffers asks us to believe that man must be complacent about corruption and look toward the good instead. That the "hawk-flights of God" are "solitary" speaks to the cynicism of Jeffers' bidding.

The effect of Jeffers' polemic on the art of his poetry is reflected in the unevenness of this poem. The first three lines (down to "look at science") and the last phrase ("if man's back holds") are prosaic and preachy as compared with the more poetic middle lines. The use of "you" has the effect of personalizing the poem, bringing an immediacy as well as a temporality to what is otherwise a rather universal and generalized discussion. The poet effectively involves the reader in the circumstances of the inhumanist's world view. With this sense of responsibility the reader is much more likely to be impressed with what Jeffers has to say.

Jeffers' advocacy of natural evolution tells in his naturalistic bent. Nature is God's agent, and in this case, the poet does not focus on God; he is much more interested in the agents. The "solitary hawk-flights of God" speaks to the romantic impulse placing all things as manifestations of God. The hawk imagery crosses nature with the "ethereal motion which is God."

A number of the excised poems contain extensive commentary on the relationship of science to man's responsibility to "seek truth." Indeed, the search for truth is an important theme that *The Double Axe* poems only suggest:[7]

Observe also
How rapidly civilization coarsens and decays; its better
qualities, foresight, humaneness, disinterested
Respect for truth, die first; its worst will be last.

The poem, "Curb Science?" comments, in part, on a point made in "Staggering Back Toward Life." In that work Jeffers noted that science was operative even if the motives of the people using the results of scientific enterprise were dishonorable and immoral. In "Curb Science?" Jeffers moves to justify the continued pursuit of knowledge with two premises: first, that "science . . . gives man hope"; and second, that science, as truth, should be an end in itself. Somewhat dogmatically, the poet rationalizes his premises thus:

To seek the truth is better than good works,
better than survival,
Holier than innocence and higher than love.

The reader is to assume, then, that the search for truth, as the goal of science, is "better," "holier," and "higher" than "good works," "survival," "innocence," and "love." This aspect of inhumanism preaches a tough-minded philosophical idealism that asks man to transcend what may be a natural impulse. This is the reasonable detachment the poet seeks as a basis of conduct, rather than passion, fanaticism, and wild hopes.

Curb Science?

Science, that gives man hope to live without lies
Or blast himself off the earth: Curb science
Until morality catches up?—But look: morality
At present running rapidly retrograde,
You'd have to turn science too, back to the witch-doctors
And myth-drunkards. Besides that morality
Is not an end in itself: truth is an end.
To seek the truth is better than good works, better than survival,
Holier than innocence and higher than love.

Science has thrust man into the future, leaving his moral
sensibilities to catch up; but that is no reason to abandon or
curb scientific pursuits. Man's moral sensibilities, which are
"running rapidly retrograde," must be made to catch up. He
must develop a truly moral, in Jeffers' sense of the word,
perspective of himself and his role in the cosmos. The
inhumanist believes that with morality in a primitive state,
science nevertheless must remain free to progress, giving man
"hope to live without lies / Or blast himself off the earth."

War-Guilt Trials
(November '45)

The mumble-jumble drones on, the hangman waits; the shabby survivin
Leaders of German are to learn that Vae Victis
Means Weh den Gesiegten. This kind of thing may console the distresses
Of Europeans: but for us! —Also we've caught
A poet, a small shrill man like a twilight bat,
Accused of being a traitor to his country. I have a bat in my tower
that knows more about treason, and about her country.

76

In *The Double Axe and Other Poems* there are verses that draw the poet's postwar thoughts. He speaks of "the triumph of the little men,"[8] and of the mystery in a universe that tolerates the energies of man. Singularly, in the excised poem "War-Guilt Trials," Jeffers writes of man prosecuting man. In this poem Jeffers makes the point that our calling to account those military and civilian leaders of the Axis powers to pay for the atrocities of the war was hardly consoling and much less satisfying. Retribution will hardly put a stop to war; indeed, retribution is "civilized" war imposed by man's justice.

"The mumble-jumble drones on" as the legalistic and, it is hoped, logical gestures of the trials become a primitive ritual in which "mumble-jumble" magically presumes to neutralize the horror behind the war makers. The monotony implied by "drones on" and the incoherence suggested by "mumble-jumble" point to the poet's feelings toward the proceedings. The postwar passion and propaganda flow on as the bombers flew, with the same low-sounding rumbling and dreary, wearing consistency. The effect of the war-guilt trials parallels the mechanical and routine act of war: both reduce the lives of men to subhuman.

Just as war achieves death and destruction, more is imminent; the predictable outcome of the trials is that "the hangman waits; the shabby surviving leaders of Germany" are to be executed.

Jeffers uses the Latin phrase "vae victis," "woe to the vanquished," to comment cynically on what he felt to be the glorious intentions of the Germans in war and to show them as historicists. There is irony in the use of the dead language of the conqueror Romans, and the poet's use of the German language in the phrase "weh den geisiegten," "too bad for the conquered," brings the reader from the romance of the past to the reality of the present. Jeffers makes the point that between Caesar's Rome and Hitler's Berlin man has had ample opportunity to learn from his mistakes. With this comparison in mind, he comments on man's behavior to impress upon him the futility of solipsistic activities. The ritual of the war-guilt trials "may console the distresses [*sic*] of Europeans," but for the American people, there can be no consolation. Here, as in other poems, Jeffers speaks of the distant interests America has had in war and of our needless participation.

Jeffers uses the word "but" ambiguously to comment on our relationship to the events at hand. The poet may be telling the reader that the trials would console the Europeans "but" for us; that we may, by our interference, lessen their value. Conversely, he may be exclaiming the trials to be merely a matter of form for the Europeans and that despite whatever satisfaction is gained, the Americans, whose country was never attacked, cannot take the same satisfaction. We must, then, find a scapegoat. And we have: "we've caught a poet." The reference is to Ezra Pound, who, because of his support of the fascists in radio broadcats in World War II, was returned to the United States from Rapello, Italy, where he had been living since 1924. Instead of standing trial for treason, Pound was committed to a federal insane asylum. In referring to Pound as a "small shrill man," Jeffers implies Pound's piercing evaluation of America's war efforts. Using a simile, "like a twilight bat," Jeffers invokes the poetic mode: the bat works not in total darkness but in that deceiving time before dusk, and thus would have to rely on special senses to avoid danger and to survive even somewhat satisfactorily. But the bat does have vision, and so it is with the poet who works with special vision. When Jeffers later personalizes the reference, "I have a bat in my tower," he is saying that he too is crazy. The metaphor speaks to the obsession of the poet-prophet. The bat illustrates the "insane" (batty?) aspects of his thoughts; it refers to the diabolic; and it refers to that innocence in nature that projects an evil image. The tower is a symbol for the mind and the heights to which man could raise himself. It symbolizes ascent and Jeffers, who himself built a tower, acknowledges a "bat," a dark being, within it. The perfect vision of the bat is gained not by sight at all but by the emanation of sound, which is broadcast like the poet's voice protesting the hazardous paths man has taken. Ezra Pound misjudged the reaction of his countrymen; Robinson Jeffers may have fallen by the same axe.

In *The Double Axe* poem, "So Many Blood-Lakes,"[9] Jeffers comments:

> *It is a foolish*
> *business to see the future and screech at it.*
> *One should watch and not speak.*

The excised poem, "The Blood-Guilt," picks up this comment and relates the history of Jeffers' protestations to war. It is a poem about the agony of the inhumanist. At a moment of self-challenge, a dialogue of Jeffers' own rigid stand—as a human being—appears. The prophetic poet debates the observations of an alter ego, who intimates the futility of such protestations yet ambiguously accuses the poet of not having the endurance or, perhaps, the slightest chance of preventing such blood-guilt.

"So long having foreseen these convulsions," begins the alter ego. The reader's immediate response is a sense of duration, both of the poet-seer's vision and of the persistence of the cause of his afflictions. Jeffers predicates a number of his suppositions on natural law: survival of the fittest. Carried to a point exhibited too often, a point beyond mere reasoning, survival requires brute force and its correlatives: conflict and

The Blood-Guilt
(February, 1944)

So long having foreseen these convulsions, forecast the hemorrhagic
Fevers of civilization past prime, striving to die, and having through
    verse, image and fable
For more than twenty years tried to condition the mind to this bloody
    climate:
    —*how* <u>*do*</u> *you* <u>*like*</u> <u>*it*</u>,
Justified prophet?
        <u>*I would rather have died twenty years ago*</u>.
                       "sad sons of
    the stormy fall,"
You said, "no escape, you have to inflict and endure . . . and the world i
    like a flight of swans."
            <u>*I said, "No escape.*</u>"
You knew also that your own country, though ocean-guarded, nothing t
    gain,
    by its destined ~~feels~~ leaders
Would be lugged in.
    I said, "No escape."
          If you had not been beaten beforehand,
    hopelessly
    ~~helplessly~~ fatalist,
You might have spoken louder and perhaps been heard, and prevented
    something.
    <u>*I*</u>? <u>*Have you never heard*</u>
<u>*That who'd lead must not see?*</u>
        You saw it, you despaired of preventing it,
    you share the blood-guilt.
                    <u>*Yes*</u>.

corruption. Jeffers' poetry then asks why man goes beyond his own capacities. Through the use of twin personnae, Jeffers is asking himself as a poet how he has persisted through years of apparently fruitless endeavor. The phrase "so long" suggests the monotonous frustration that has been the only consequence of his foretelling and foreseeing. The phrase also ambiguously reflects the alter ego's sweep from past to present; he notes that the poet should have (and now, finally, has) said "goodbye" to his efforts and hopes of alerting mankind.

Man's illness manifests severe "convulsions," hemorrhagic fevers, and a death wish. In this metaphor Jeffers describes his concept of civilization. The wagging, the imbalance connoted by "convulsions," is typical of Jeffers as he insists that the acts of man are like those of a naive and impressionable child or those of a doddering old fool resigned to indecision when not following his more aggressive tendencies. Man's essential being is ruptured when he denies its natural inclination or prostitutes it to the machinations and horrors of war. Ironically, the fevers of such loss bring man to a hellish state where fluctuating temperatures and indecision in civilized actions show human existence to be undesirable. Man finds himself "striving to die" because in death there is at least certainty and, perhaps, natural solace.

As inhumanist, Jeffers is the prophetic poet who admits to his design "to condition the mind" of his civilization to the incongruities of its "climate." The poet is, in effect, setting his conscience in order, and the reader can detect a subdued sense of sorrow. The word Yes at the end of the poem is Jeffers' admission of a share of the blood-guilt. The poem sets up an interesting dichotomy: the prophet and the resigned perpetrator, the accused and the guilty. But the guilt is of the general kind; even the accusor is, in a sense, guilty.

Wilson in Hell
(Written in 1942)

Roosevelt died and met Wilson; who said, "I blundered into it
Through honest error, and conscience cut me so deep that I died
In the vain effort to prevent future wars. But you
Blew on the coal-bed, and when it kindled you deliberately
Sabotaged every fire-wall that even the men who denied
My hope had built. You have too much murder on your hands. I will not
Speak of the lies and connivings. I cannot understand the Mercy
That permits us to meet in the same heaven. —Or is this my hell?"

"Wilson in Hell" is a very damning poem, much like a spite-
ful tragic satire. It refers to President Roosevelt as a saboteur
and calls him a traitor. Compared with the other excised
poems, "Wilson in Hell" is blatantly inflammatory. Jeffers
presents the spirit of President Roosevelt to the spirit of
President Wilson. In this theoretical meeting, Wilson reviews
the efforts of both as they guided a people through war.
Wilson offers an apologia, revealing the frustration he felt:
"conscience cut me so deep that I died." Only now in death
can he admit to the futility of seeking "to prevent future
wars." As Wilson's remarks turn toward Roosevelt's efforts,
Jeffers uses a double-edged metaphor:

> *you [Roosevelt]*
> *Blew on the coal-bed, and when it kindled you deliberately*
> *Sabotaged every fire-wall.*

The "coal-bed" is the specific political situation that is a
metaphoric particular of the larger human condition as Jeffers
sees it. In this context, Roosevelt is likened to the wind, itself
of little substance but of considerable effect. The "coal-bed" is
also suggestive of the hell to which Wilson suspects he has

fallen (having failed to bring about peace). Logically then, the man who intensifies this earthly hell by blowing on it is Satan's counterpart. The word "Sabotaged" is consistent with this satanic activity; thus, when Wilson declares Roosevelt a saboteur, he thematically links this poem with "Miching Mallecho," which deals with sneaking mischief and sabotage. The irony of the ending comments on Wilson's defense of his tenure as leader of the people. Wilson's good may contravene God's will as much as did Roosevelt's "evil." Building fire-walls for peace, that is, may be as out of line with God's grand design as is blowing on coal-beds.

In this poem Jeffers' problem was where to put a man, retributively, whom he somewhat admired, and where to put a man, retributively, whom he disliked. Jeffers undercut Roosevelt by putting Wilson in hell—as if by afterthought ("Or is this my hell?"). The title, then, seems preconceived. Compared with Roosevelt, who, according to Jeffers, belongs in hell, Wilson probably was conceived of as belonging in heaven.

The artistic accomplishments of the excised poems are varied. In an attempt to impress his readers with a particular world view, Jeffers wrote intensely, demanding of them a difficult task: to cultivate a perspective of man that puts man in his true place in the grand cosmos. In these poems Jeffers anticipated the future of mankind, recognizing that only with change will the human race be able to endure and cope with the future. Jeffers saw, in the cosmic harmony that holds all things in a cohesive and evolving whole, the constant upon which man could rely. An awareness of and reliance on this larger harmony was essential if civilization was to adapt and perpetuate itself. The excised poems reveal a cynical Jeffers who dealt with a naturalistic fatalism even more pronounced and inescapable than was shown in the published poems.

Asking man to acknowledge decadence, Jeffers depicted—
often with brutal particularity—"civilization decaying and
sick." The excised poems, imperfect as some of them are,
pointed the way of the inhumanist who would arrest man's
self-destruction. Bewilderment, outrage, apology, and polemic were the stuff of these assertions; sometimes they were
shaped into poetry, sometimes not.

But it was not on the grounds of artistic merit that Random
House asked Jeffers to delete these ten poems and to alter
others. The sharpness of *The Double Axe,* one might say, was
blunted—its most pointed poems and metaphors softened for
political, not aesthetic reasons.

5.

THE PARABLE OF THE WATER

A most puzzling question is why Jeffers allowed the ten poems to be excised from his original manuscript. In this day when artistic license is defended in so many quarters, it seems curious that a man with such strong convictions would permit his work to be altered so radically. The logical explanation seems to be that Jeffers gave in to editorial judgment as a function of his inhumanism. Peace of mind was an imperative for him and went far to explain his acquiescence in the matter. He deferred as naturally to Saxe Commins' judgment as, in his view, a rock defers to the erosion of the waves. As he wrote, again in third person,[1]

Jeffers says that he has felt some degree of liking, or at least pity, for every person he has ever met; but his emotions have never been engaged by mankind in general. His attitude toward the human race is an intellectual attitude. He just doesn't think that humanity (himself included) amounts to much.

This is one source of "peace of mind." If you don't expect much you are never much disappointed.

This disillusionment on the subject of human values has left Jeffers comparatively unambitious; and certainly non-competitive. This is another course of "peace of mind."

A third source is his confidence in universal nature — not in nature's kindness but in nature's beauty.

He has a mystical feeling toward this natural beauty; it seems to him to be the essence or the shining-forth of some essential value — a value beyond human reference — a divineness in nature. There will probably be other minds and senses — probably better made than ours — to admire it; but he feels that admired or not, it will still be beautiful.

Jeffers could see no use in trying to pacify his editor. This, of course, was entirely compatible with the poet's philosophical stance. He did not compromise; he believed that each man had a right to act in accordance with the dictates of his conscience.

Given Jeffers' beliefs, it seems remarkable that he actually did alter substantially two of the poems that were published; "Quia Absurdum" and "Historical Choice." There is no accounting for his decision to rework these two poems and not the ten that were ultimately excised: "I Pearl Harbor," "II West Coast Blackout," "Eve of Invasion," "New Year's Dawn," "Inquisitors," and "Mamouth" also were altered but not significantly.[2] The changes in "Quia Absurdum" and "Historical Choice" are, however, revealing and suggest what Jeffers could have done to the deleted poems had he cared to.

Quia Absurdum

Guard yourself from the terrible empty light of
    space, the bottomless
Pool of the stars. (Expose yourself to it: you might learn
    something.)
Guard yourself from perceiving the inherent nastiness of
    man and woman.
(Expose your mind to it: you might learn something.)
Faith, as they now confess, is preposterous, an act of will.
    Choose the Christian sheep-cote
        <u>*rat-pack*</u>*:* <u>*faith*</u> <u>*will*</u> <u>*protect*</u> <u>*you*</u> *from* <u>*the*</u>
Or the Communist rat-fight: faith will cover your head
    <u>*pool*</u> <u>*of*</u> <u>*stars*</u>*.*
    from the man-devouring stars.

Where the text of the original version differs from that of the published version the original is above the published and is underlined.

"Quia Absurdum" is about faith. Religion, whether Christianity or Communism, was a drug; faith would "cover your head." In changing "rat-pack" to "rat-fight," Jeffers removed from Communism the ideological homogeneity and communal harmony implied in the word "pack." These characteristics were implied also in the word "sheep," used in reference to Christianity. The change set up a polarity in which Christianity and Communism were madly caught up in a struggle for survival, a "rat-fight." In either case, the poet believed that blind and exclusive belief was a crutch; "Faith will cover your head" might be read "close your eyes and reality will pass away." Perhaps, more sadly, blind faith hindered man from realizing the true nature of the universe: in the final analysis, "The man-devouring stars" surely would be more consequential than egocentric humanity.

Jeffers's original version read much more gently. Faith, traditionally, would "protect" one; the "pool of stars" combined looking down into a pool and looking up at the "stars." The indifference of "pool" was replaced by the hostile adjective, "man-devouring." To cover one's head with the blanket of faith—given the inescapable hostility of the universe—was, to cite the poem's title, patently absurd.

The changes in this poem reflected Jeffers' desire to impress upon the reader the intensity of the battle man must fight with himself. Therefore, he used a battle metaphor, in which "fight" and "devouring" replaced merely descriptive terms.

The changes in "Historical Choice," however, were even more pronounced than those in "Quia Absurdum." Instead of strengthening its message, Jeffers sought to tone down the poem's most pointed and blatant accusations. For this reason especially, the poem was unique.

Historical Choice
(*Written in 1943*)

Strong enough to be neutral—as is now proved,
    while
    now American power
                fogs,
From Australia to the Aleutian fog-seas, and Hawaii to

    Africa, rides every wind—we were misguided by
    fear and fraud and a great tricky leader's
By fraud and fear, by our public fools and a loved leader's
        orotund cajoleries,
        ambition,

To meddle in the fever-dreams of decaying Europe. We

    could have forced peace, even when France fell;

        we chose
        take sides
To make alliance and feed war.

Actum Est. There is no returning now.
Two bloody summers from now (I suppose) we shall have
to take up the corrupting burden and curse of
victory.

<u>split in council</u>
We shall have to hold half the earth; we shall be sick with
<u>at home</u>.
self-disgust,
<u>thoroughly hated abroad</u>.
And hated by friend and foe, and hold half the earth—

or let it go, and go down with it. Here is a burden
<u>for: we are not like the ancient Romans</u>,
We are not fit for. We are not like Romans and Britons—
natural world-rulers,
Bullies by instinct—but we have to bear it. Who has kissed
Fate on the mouth, and blown out the lamp—must
lie with her.

Where the text of the original version differs from that of the published version the original is above the published and is underlined.

In changing "by fear and fraud and a great tricky leader's / orotund cajoleries" to "by fraud and fear, by our public fools and a loved leader's / ambition," Jeffers deflected the attack on Roosevelt and his political program and cynically and ironically described the president as a "loved leader." The theme of deception in "tricky" was not lost; the reversal of "fear and fraud" to "fraud and fear" emphasized the "miching mallecho," which Jeffers supposed to be characteristic of Roosevelt's political strategy. The syntactical change made even more forceful the irony of "loved leader" juxtaposed to "our public fools."

By using "ambition" for "orotund cajoleries" the poet deemphasized the suggestion made previously that the president was a political puppet who offered only "democratic gestures." This placed the burden of what, in context, amounted to a manic obsession for personal achievement, "ambition," on the man himself and was consistent with the view of Roosevelt manifest in the poem "Wilson's Hell." The published last line of the first stanza, "to make alliance and feed war," exposed the sophisticated devices of the diplomat and politician.

The original line "to take sides and feed war" pointed up the childish and arbitrary act of war-as-game. This, of course, in part excused the man's act as determined and premeditated rather than whimsical and selfish.

The principal change in the second stanza, to "we shall be sick with / self-disgust, / and hated by friend and foe," from "we shall be split in council / at home / And thoroughly hated abroad," pointed up the incestuous and egocentric deterioration, "self-disgust," that "split council" did not connote. To say that we would be "hated by friend and foe" rather than be "thoroughly hated abroad" was to say that we would be completely alone, each in himself, apart from the universe.

In the published version Jeffers also dropped the modifier "ancient" when describing the "Romans," and added "Britons." The result brought the cynicism and meaning of the poem into a more immediate context, and the American reader was more likely to respond personally with the British brought into the picture. The relationship of these empires to America was further reinforced with the use of "we."

The world view of inhumanism addressed the paradox of creation in many of its circumstances. Here was man given over to war because of energies that did not have the power to mediate, yet without which he was not man. Here was a poet who would seek peace by pointing up the terrible and passionate involvements of man. This poet claimed an "attitude toward the human race" that was intellectual; yet his poetry involved man emotionally, both as subject and as reader. Among Jeffers' papers was a holograph, "Statement of philosophic viewpoint," that addressed the paradox. Again he wrote in the third person:[3]

Jeffers has been accused of confusion and self-contradiction. He says that it may be true on occasion—for who is not?—but often the self-contradiction is only apparent. Things have different aspects at different levels of contemplation, and all these aspects may be true. War, for instance, is horrible, disgusting, heroic, ridiculous, futile and necessary, destructive and creative, ugly as hell, tragically and spectacularly beautiful—all according to the levels from which you consider it. (Politicians "ought" not to contradict themselves; but poets may, and still speak the truth.)

Again, Jeffers regards the human race as almost infinitely unimportant in the universe; but he knows that it is essential in his business—poetry—and this causes appearances of self-contradiction that he sometimes has labored greatly to explain. He says in one of his shorter poems (Soliloquy in February) that he is determined to tell the truth in poetry "—I can tell lies in prose."

Thus Jeffers saw "confusion and self-contradiction" as natural to man—especially to a poet writing of man from "different levels of contemplation." When Jeffers agreed to delete some of the *Double Axe* poems and alter others, he arbitrarily but naturally pointed up the inconsistency of men's acts.

One cannot help but wonder, then, about the apparent narrowness of scope of *The Double Axe*. Where were the "different levels of contemplation?" The intensity of Jeffers' philosophy all but blotted out the naturalistic and human(e) passages that addressed the quality of life this planet possibly might enjoy—even in a Jeffersian world. But there were other books of poems: the Carmel narratives, for example, in which

Jeffers wrote of people participating in passionate dramas along the coastal range. There were the sonnets and odes that sang descriptions of nature and of plain people. Perhaps what is most difficult is recognizing that as a poet, Jeffers' perceptions grew as he lived each day. Eventually, he came to realize that all was not as it should be with his fellow man and this, coupled with Jeffers' determination to "tell the truth," made his poetry become increasingly stark.

The experience of *The Double Axe* manuscript encapsulated a moment in Jeffers' history as a poet. Some of the poems were moving and well shaped; others were not. The war metaphors lent immediacy to what Jeffers would have man realize. But Jeffers seemed to have been fighting a losing battle, and perhaps he finally realized it. Man did not want to hear the hawk's cry; and, above all, man did not seem to want Jeffers to apply his incriminating view of mankind to contemporary, popular figures.

But Jeffers continued to attempt to preach his view of the universe by pointing up the fantastic and temporary expedients by which contemporary, as well as historical man, lived. Seven years after *The Double Axe* was published, Jeffers received this letter from Saxe Commins:[4]

APRIL 2, 1953

MR. ROBINSON JEFFERS
ROUTE 2, BOX 36
CARMEL, CALIFORNIA

DEAR ROBIN;

THE TWO POEMS FOLLOWED UPON YOUR LETTER BY ONE DAY. I AM ACKNOWLEDGING THEM BOTH. I QUITE AGREE THAT "THE DEER" WOULD MAKE A MARVELLOUS CODA FOR YOUR BOOK. MY

OWN INCLINATION IS TO KEEP "OCEAN" AND PLACE IT JUST BEFORE "SKUNKS." AS TO THAT POEM WITH ITS MALODOROUS TITLE, I WOULD LIKE TO MAKE A SUGGESTION IF I MAY. IT SEEMS TO ME THAT YOUR POINT IS DULLED BY THE POLITICAL IMPLICATIONS IN THE REFERENCE TO HITLER, STALIN AND ROOSEVELT. MY OWN INCLINATION WOULD BE TO OMIT THE LINES "LET US NOT SPEAK OF HITLER, STALIN AND ROOSEVELT FOR A HUNDRED YEARS AND THEY'LL BE HARMLESS UNDAMNED ABSTRACTIONS." INSTEAD, I WOULD LIKE TO SUGGEST THAT FOLLOWING THE WORDS "A GREAT AUTHOR OF TRAGEDIES" YOU MIGHT KEEP IT IN THE PAST BY THE FOLLOWING, "FOR CENTURES THEY WILL BE HARMLESS, UNDAMNED ABSTRACTIONS." THIS CHANGE, IT SEEMS TO ME, MAKES THE POINT OF THE POEM ANNOUNCED IN THE LAST THREE WORDS, "DISTANCE MAKES CLEAN," REALLY EFFECTIVE. I'M VERY ANXIOUS TO KNOW HOW YOU FEEL ABOUT THIS.

LOVE,
SAXE

The book of which Saxe Commins wrote was *Hungerfield and Other Poems,* published by Random House in 1953. It was Jeffer's first book since *The Double Axe* and his last completed book before he died in 1962. Apparently, Robinson Jeffers' battle to enunciate his world view continued even after the thumping that *The Double Axe* received in the late forties.

The difficulty of Jeffers' art lay in its union of an ego-denying doctrine and a passionate poet who demanded specific metaphors. To see the world of an inhumanist's poem, one must allow for a time that all did not revolve about man's earth. Mankind was not in and of itself a monument to its own peculiar and singular prowess. Ranging from Copernicus to Darwin, Jeffers would have argued, the lessons of the great men of history indicated that man was but part of a larger plan. Only in aspiration, in "transhuman magnificence," could the race continue. For Jeffers, the *race* was not won; it was, instead, superseded.

CHRONOLOGY

*10 January 1887	John Robinson Jeffers, born to Dr. William Hamilton Jeffers, A.B., D.D., LL.D. (1838-1914) and to Annie Tuttle Jeffers (1860-1921) in Allegheny, Pennsylvania.
January 1888	Family moves to Sewickley, Pennsylvania.
Summers, 1891 and 1892	In Europe with parents: concerts and galleries.
22 June 1891	Kindergarten in Zurich.
June 1892	Kindergarten in Lucerne.
October 1893	Family moves to Edgeworth.
1894	Birth of Hamilton Jeffers.
23 August 1897	John Robinson Jeffers writes first letter; addressed to his father.
1898-1901	European schools: Aleipzig Day School; Villa La Tour at Vevey; Chateau de Vidy at Lausanne; the Pension at International Thudichym at Geneva; Villa Erika at Zurich.
1902	University of Western Pennsylvania (University of Pittsburgh).
1903	Moves to Long Beach, California.
1903	Moves to Highland Park, California. Attends Occidental College.

*Asterisks indicate occasions of special significance. (For additional information concerning works published, see References.)

1903-07	Publishes thirteen poems.
1903	Moves to Manhattan Beach, California.
1904	Named editor of *The Occidental*.
*June 1904	*The Youth's Companion* publishes "The Condor" (first poem for which Jeffers is paid).
15 June 1904	Receives bachelor's degree.
1905	Enrolls in the University of Southern California. Publishes in the USC literary magazine, the *University Courier*. Meets Mrs. Una Call Kuster in a German class.
27 April 1906	Enters the University of Zurich.
September 1907	Enters USC Medical School.
August 1910	Enters the University of Washington School of Forestry.
*4 December 1912	*Flagon and Apples* (Grafton Publishing Company, Los Angeles) is printed.
12 January 1913	Receives a legacy from a cousin of maternal grandfather, John F. Robinson.
*2 August 1913	Marries Una Call Kuster in Tacoma, Washington.
5 May 1914	Birth of Jeffers' first child, Maeve, who dies one day later.
*September 1914	Moves to Carmel-By-the-Sea, California.
20 December 1914	Death of Dr. William Hamilton Jeffers.
*11 October 1916	Macmillan Company publishes *Californians*.
*9 November 1916	Birth of twin boys, Donnan and Garth.
15 August 1919	Moves into Tor House on Mission Point, Carmel.
*April 1924	Peter G. Boyle prints *Tamar and Other Poems*.

June 1925	The Book Club of California publishes an anthology edited by J. H. Jackson, *Continent's End*. The Title poem was by Jeffers.
*10 November 1925	Boni and Liveright publish *Roan Stallion, Tamar and Other Poems*.
1 April 1927	*The Advance* publishes Jeffers' review of James Rorty's *Children of the Sun and Other Poems*.
*30 June 1927	Boni and Liveright publish *The Women At Point Sur*.
October 1928	The Book Club of California has the Grabhorn Press print *Poems,* with an introduction by Benjamin H. Lehman.
November 1928	John S. Mayfield privately publishes *An Artist*.
1928	John S. Mayfield privately publishes "Robinson Jeffers: Tragic Terror," by Benjamin De Casseves. (It also appears in *Bookman,* vol. 66, November 1927, pp. 262-66).
*19 November 1928	Horace Liveright publishes *Cawdor and Other Poems*.
2 December 1928	The *New York Herald Tribune* publishes Jeffers' review of Mark Van Doren's *Now The Sky and Other Poems*.
June 1929	The Jeffers go to Ireland, where they remained until December 10.
*16 November 1929	Horace Liveright publishes *Dear Judas and Other Poems*.
February 1930	The Flame Press publishes "Stars."
June 1930	With Mabel Dodge Luhan in Taos, New Mexico. (The family made long summer trips here in 1933, 1934, 1935, 1937, and 1938.)

December 1930	Harry Ward Ritchie, Paris, publishes "Apology for Bad Dreams."
5 March 1931	*The New Freeman* publishes Jeffers' review of Babette Deutsch's *Epistle to Prometheus.*
*10 December 1931	Random House publishes *Descent to the Dead.*
*26 March 1932	Liveright publishes *Thurso's Landing and Other Poems.*
1932	Mortar Board Dramatic Group of the University of California, produces *Tower Beyond Tragedy* under the direction of Edwin Duerr.
26 May 1932	"Firstbook" (prose) is published in *The Colophon:* Part X. 1933. Cultural History Research, of Rye, New York, publishes S. S. Alberts' *A Bibliography of The Works of Robinson Jeffers.*
*June 1933	Random House publishes *Give Your Heart to the Hawks* (which receives honorable mention from the Commonwealth Club of California when the club presents Literary Awards for 1933.)
*1935	Random House publishes *Solstice and Other Poems* (which in January 1937 will win the Book of the Month Club prize).
January 1937	The National Institute of Arts and Letters elects Jeffers to membership.
January 1937	Occidental College confers on Jeffers the honorary degree of Doctor of Humane Letters.
*1937	Random House publishes *Such Counsels You Gave to Me.*

1937	Quercus Press, San Mateo, California, publishes "Hope is not for the Wise" (folio).
June 1937	Travels to Ireland and to Europe, returning October 30.
*April 1938	Random House publishes *The Selected Poetry of Robinson Jeffers*.
December 1939	Quercus Press publishes *The Condor* (folio) and *Two Consolations* (broadside).
1940	Jeffers elected to honorary membership in Phi Beta Kappa.
February 1941	Accepts an invitation from the Library of Congress in Washington, D.C., to inaugurate a Poetry Series in Washington, Pittsburgh, Princeton, Cambridge, New York, Buffalo, Indianapolis, Kansas City, and Salt Lake City.
*1941	Random House publishes *Be Angry at the Sun*.
July 1941	John Gassner adapts Jeffers' "Tower Beyond Tragedy" for a production at the open-air forest theatre in Carmel. Dame Judith Anderson plays the lead, Clytemnestra.
November 1945	Declines an invitation to represent the Pacific Coast in the Academy of American Poets.
November, 1945	Elected to membership in the American Academy of Arts and Letters.
*July 1946	Random House Publishes *Medea*.
August 1947	Michael Myerberg stages Jeffers' *Dear Judas* (which is banned in Boston).

1947	The National Theatre stages *Medea* (Dame Judith Anderson, for whom the play was adapted, plays the lead).
*January 1948	Random House publishes *The Double Axe and Other Poems*.
1948	Ward Ritchie Press, Los Angeles, publishes "Poetry, Gongorism and A Thousand Years" (originally printed in the *New York Times Magazine,* January 18, 1948).
June 1948	The Jeffers go to Ireland (where Jeffers becomes seriously ill).
*September 1950	Death of Una.
November 1950	The American National Theatre and Academy opens its winter series with *Tower Beyond Tragedy*. (Dame Judith Anderson plays the lead.)
1951	Receives the Eunice Tietjens Memorial Prize for a group of poems that appears in *Poetry Magazine*.
December 1952	Grabhorn Press publishes privately *Hungerfield*.
*July 1954	Random House publishes *Hungerfield and Other Poems*.
May 1954	The Arena Stage in Washington, D.C., produces *The Cretan Woman*.
1954	Edits Una's diaries, *Visits to Ireland,* published by Theodore Lilienthal, printed by Ward Ritchie Press.
1955	Receives the Borestone Mountain Poetry Award for *Hungerfield*.
Summer 1955	Stanford University produces *The Cretan Woman*.

*May 1956	The Book Club of California publishes *Themes In My Poems*.
1956	Jeffers' last trip to Ireland.
1956	Merle Armitage and the Ward Ritchie Press publish "The Loving Shepherdess," illustrated by Jean Kellogg.
1958	Receives award from the Academy of American Poets.
1961	Receives the Shelly Memorial Award presented by the National Poetry Society.
*20 January 1962	At the age of 75, John Robinson Jeffers dies in his sleep at Tor House, Carmel-By-the-Sea, California.
*1963	Random House publishes *The Beginning and the End*.
1963	Random House, Vintage Books, publishes *Robinson Jeffers, Selected Poems*.
1971	Scrimshaw Press publishes *Jeffers Country: the Seed Plots of Robinson Jeffers' Poetry* (Jeffers' poetry and the photography of Horace Lyon).
1971	Cayucos Books publishes *Californians* (A reissue with an introduction by William Everson).
*1973	Cayucos Books publishes *The Alpine Christ and Other Poems*. (poems and other writings meant for a book never published; with commentary and notes by William Everson).

NOTES

CHAPTER 1

1. Robinson Jeffers, *The Double Axe and Other Poems* (New York: Random House, 1948).

2. Jeffers, *The Double Axe,* p. 53.

3. Melba Berry Bennett, *The Stone Mason of Tor House* (Menlo Park, Calif.: Ward Ritchie Press, 1966), p. 66.

4. As Una explained to Melba Berry Bennett, "Without the wish of either of us our life was one of those fatal attractions that happened unplanned and undesired. We both hated for our families the unwelcome publicity of divorce" (Bennett, *Stone Mason of Tor House,* p. 47). The Los Angeles papers played up the divorce with headlines and pictures. On February 28, 1913, headlines read, "Love's Gentle Alchemy to Weld Broken Lives"; on March 1, 1913, the *Los Angeles Times* carried Robin's and Una's pictures with the headlines "Two Points of the Eternal Triangle" and "Parents Wash Hands of It."

5. Ibid., p. 69.

6. Robinson Jeffers, Jeffers Collection, Humanities Research Center, University of Texas, Austin, hereinafter Jeffers Collection.

7. Robinson Jeffers, Jeffers Collection.

8. As Bennett has observed, "Una was often criticized because she zealously protected her husband." Knowledge of the vigor of Una's feelings bore heavily on the poet; he felt it keenly (Bennett, p. 121).

9. Local Board for Monterey County, Salinas, California, "Red Ink Serial Number 2060, Local Order Number 1529."

10. Robinson Jeffers, Jeffers Collection.

11. Bennett, *Stone Mason of Tor House,* p. 86.

12. Robinson Jeffers. Jeffers Collection (italics mine). The cancelled lines are as they appear in the notes, changed by Jeffers in his own hand.

13. Robinson Jeffers, foreword to *The Selected Poetry of Robinson Jeffers,* 1st ed. (New York: Random House, 1937), p. xiv.

14. Jeffers, *Selected Poetry,* p. xv.

15. B. H. Lehman, foreword to Robinson Jeffers, *Themes in My Poems* (San Francisco: Book Club of California, 1956), p. vi.

16. Jeffers, *Themes in My Poems,* p. viii.

17. Ibid., p. 13.

18. Robinson Jeffers, "What Odd Expedients," Jeffers Collection.

19. Robinson Jeffers, "The Love and the Hate," *The Double Axe and Other Poems* (New York: Random House, 1948), p. 49.

20. Robinson Jeffers, "Untitled Poem," Jeffers Collection.

21. Robinson Jeffers, *Themes in My Poems* (San Francisco: Book Club of California, 1956), p. 46.

22. Robinson Jeffers, "Preface," Jeffers Collection.

23. Robinson Jeffers, Jeffers Collection.

24. Jeffers, *The Double Axe,* p. 105.

25. Robinson Jeffers, Jeffers Collection.

CHAPTER 2

1. Robinson Jeffers, "The Day Is a Poem," in *Be Angry at the Sun and Other Poems* (New York: Random House, 1941), p. 126.

2. Robinson Jeffers, *Themes in My Poems* (San Francisco: Book Club of California, 1956), p. 46.

3. Robinson Jeffers, *The Double Axe and Other Poems* (New York: Random House, 1948), p. vii.

4. Warren Allen Smith, "Authors and Humanism," *Humanist* 11 (October 1951): 193-204.

5. Lawrence Clark Powell, *Robinson Jeffers, The Man and His Work* (Pasadena, Calif.: San Pasqual Press, 1940), p. 209.

6. Mercedes Cunningham Monjian, *Robinson Jeffers: A Study in Inhumanism* (Pittsburgh: University of Pittsburgh Press, 1958).

7. Robinson Jeffers, "Margrave," *Thurso's Landing* (New York: Liveright, 1932), pp. 135-36.

8. Jeffers, *Thurso's Landing,* p. 141.

9. Hyatt Howe Waggoner, "Robinson Jeffers: Here is Reality," *The Heel of Elohim: Science and Values in Modern American Poetry* (Norman: University of Oklahoma Press, 1950), p. 131.

10. Radcliffe Squires, *The Loyalties of Robinson Jeffers* (Ann Arbor: University of Michigan Press, 1956), pp. 31-32.

11. Squires, *Loyalties of Robinson Jeffers,* p. 120.

12. Ibid., p. 127.

13. Jeffers, "The Place for No Story," *Selected Poetry,* p. 356.

14. Jeffers, "Praise Life," *Selected Poetry,* p. 370.

15. Jeffers, "Signpost," *Selected Poetry,* p. 374.

16. Jeffers, "Note," *Be Angry at the Sun.*

17. Jeffers, "The Answer," *Selected Poetry,* p. 594.

18. Jeffers, *Themes in My Poems,* p. 28.

CHAPTER 3

1. Robinson Jeffers, *The Double Axe and Other Poems* (New York: Random House, 1948), p. ix.

2. Ruth Lechlitner, "A Prophet of Mortality," *New York Herald Tribune Weekly Book Review,* September 12, 1948, sec. 7, p. 4, cols, 1, 2, 3.

3. Jeffers, "Preface," *The Double Axe,* p. vii.

4. Ibid., p. viii.

5. Ann N. Ridgeway, in her preface to *The Selected Letters of Robinson Jeffers, 1897-1962,* writes, "When I first proposed to assemble Robinson Jeffers' correspondence, I was warned that it was Una who wrote most letters in order to assure her husband time to write poems." Lawrence Clark Powell, in *Robinson Jeffers, The Man and His Work* (Pasadena, Calif.: San Pasqual Press, 1940), p. 28, admits that "Jeffers owes a great debt to his wife, Una. . . . All the many details of managing a house without servants are handled by her — as well as the poet's considerable 'fan-mail' — and he is left free to work."

6. Letter from Bennett Cerf to Una Jeffers, November 24, 1934, Jeffers Collection.

7. Letter from Bennett Cerf to Una Jeffers, April 21, 1938, Jeffers Collection.

8. Letter from Bennett Cerf to Una Jeffers, April 1, 1938, Jeffers Collection.

9. Saxe Commins to Robinson Jeffers, October 15, 1947, Jeffers Collection.

10. Lines 25 and 26, "page 29," of the published version. This item was changed (p. 27), but not to what Commins suggested. See Chapter 4 of this volume for Jeffers' version ("to feed the power-hunger of politicians and make trick fortunes"). Line 27, "p. 91": In "The Inhumanist," part 36, pp. 92-93, "We and the Russians Are . . . great destroyers . . . (and following). Apparently not changed by the poet.

"p. 122": Reference to expunged poem, "Fantasy."

"p. 125": Not decipherable.

"p. 126": Reference to expunged poem, "The Blood-Guilt."

"p. 129": Reference to expunged poem, "Wilson in Hell."

"p. 135": Reference to "Historical Choice," which was modified.

"p. 136": Reference to "Teheran," in which leaders, "little smiling attendants," are meeting "to plot against whom what future." Somewhat sympathetic to "Unlucky Germany." Unchanged by the poet.

"p. 137": Reference to expunged poem, "What Odd Expedients."

11. Saxe Commins to Robinson Jeffers, December 4, 1947, Jeffers Collection.

12. Saxe Commins to Robinson Jeffers, February 12, 1948, Jeffers Collection.

13. That this did occur is evidenced by such reviews as that in the *New York Herald Tribune Weekly Book Review,* September 12, 1948, p. vii.

14. Robinson Jeffers to Saxe Commins, February 19, 1948, Robinson Jeffers Letters, Random House Collection, Rare Book

and Manuscript Library, Columbia University Libraries, New York City, hereinafter Random House Collection.

15. Bennett Cerf to Una Jeffers, October 7, 1947, Jeffers Collection.

16. Bennett Cerf to Una Jeffers, March 18, 1948, Jeffers Collection.

17. Dudley Fitts, *New York Times Book Review,* August 22, 1948.

18. Reference to Kenneth Patchen, poet-novelist, 1911 —. His poetry, marked by religious symbols and intricate figures recalling the metaphysical poets, also is free in structure and associations.

19. *Time,* July 5, 1948, p. 32.

20. *Time,* August 2, 1948, pp. 79-80.

21. Ibid.

22. Gerald McDonald, *Library Journal* 73 (June 15, 1948): 948.

23. *New Yorker,* September 4, 1948, p. 75.

24. Robinson Jeffers to Saxe Commins, March 2, 1948, Random House Collection.

25. Saxe Commins to Robinson Jeffers, March 4, 1948, Random House Collection.

26. Robert Fitzgerald, *New Republic,* November 1948, p. 22.

27. Seldon Rodman, "Transhuman Magnificence," *Saturday Review of Literature,* July 31, 1948, pp. 13-14.

CHAPTER 4

On the excised poems:

"Miching Mallecho." The date (May, 1941), is as it appears on the holographic and typewritten MSS. Those poems published in *The Double Axe* and bearing dates have the words *written in* preceding the date, in parentheses.

"Miching Mallecho." *Oxford English Dictionary:* "Occurs only in the Shakesperean passage quoted and echoes of it; of uncertain form, origin and meaning. it is probable that the first word is a present participle of the verb micher: to sneak, skulk, pilfer. The second word probably represents the Spanish malheco meaning misdeed which early editors printed mallecho but was originally malicho or mallico."

"Fantasy." The date (June 1941), is as it appears on the holographic and typewritten MSS. In form it is consistent with the poems published in *The Double Axe*. Working titles: "Gunpowder Plotters," "Future Armistice Day," "Armistice Day," "Journey's End."

"The Blood-Guilt." The date is as it appears on the holographic and typewritten MSS. The typewritten MS. shows the following alterations: in 1.3, the poet wrote "story" for "fable"; in 1.16, "fools" was tried for "leaders"; in 1.20, "helplessly" was tried for "hopelessly"; the first draft (holographic) contained an additional stanze at the end:

> Buchenwald and Lidice and Bataan will not be remembered,
>   nor Hiroshima forgotten.
> Long ago, men talked peace, you said war. Now that
>   all men shout war,
>   what will you say?
>   <u>War</u>.
>   – ~~Civil War~~ –
>   – ~~Nothing~~ –

"Wilson in Hell." The date (1942), is as it appears on the typewritten MS. In form it is consistent with poems published in *The Double Axe*.

"What Odd Expedients." Working titles appearing on holographic MS: "The Solution of War," "Mourn Them Not Much," "Two Bulls in One Pasture," "Ways and Means," and "What Odd Inventions."

"Pourvou Que Ca Doure." A working title, appearing on the holographic MS, was "Look All Around You." The surviving typewritten MS bore these notations: 1.5, "dying" was considered as an alternative to "sick"; 1.7, the poet considered placing the word "once" between "had" and "sense"; 1.13, "magnificence" was considered as an alternative to "corpses"; 1.14, "fallow" was deleted, as was the phrase "—come, —storm-plows"; following after "future" and continuing into 1.15 with "be-strong,—seed," which would have preceded "if man's back holds." (However, it is uncertain whether the last phrase would have been written if the poet had not deleted the original line.)

On the chapter's text:

1. Robinson Jeffers, "Invasion," *The Double Axe and Other Poems* (New York: Random House, 1948), p. 131.

2. Jeffers, "The Double Axe, Part I, The Love and the Hate," *The Double Axe,* p. 27.

3. Ibid, p. 18.

4. Hamlet's translation clarifies the notion that, indeed, "sneaking mischief" has brought about a national tragedy. The context from which the reference comes is one of fratricide and incest: Claudius has killed his brother to take his crown and win his wife. These themes are catholic to the Jeffers canon. For the poet of inhumanism the world is caught up in itself. There is such disintegration of value as is wrought by fratricide for privilege and position. Symbolically, inbreeding weakens the race and hastens its decay—thus, another argument for that tenet of inhumanism that would have us reach out to nature and seek to participate in the grander scheme of things.

5. In the Gunpowder Plot, the plot of a few Roman Catholics to blow up the Houses of Parliament on November 5, 1605, while the King, Lords, and Commons were assembled, Guy Fawkes was chosen to execute the plan. He was betrayed and arrested on November 4. Later he was executed.

6. "Bulls." This metaphor is especially rich in its varius usages: a speculator, a bubble, a fraud or deceit, a prison guard, an iron rod used in the process of blasting. (*Oxford English Dictionary.*)

7. Robinson Jeffers, "Teheran," *The Double Axe,* p. 128.
8. Jeffers, "Greater Grandeur," *The Double Axe,* p. 139.
9. Jeffers, "So Many Blood-Lakes," *The Double Axe,* p. 132.

CHAPTER 5

1. Robinson Jeffers, Jeffers Collection.
2. "I Pearl Harbor" and "II West Coast Blackout" were merged into "Pearl Harbor," having Parts I and II.

"Eve of Invasion" became "Invasion" by the dropping of "Eve of." In the simplicity of its new title the poem becomes much more dramatic.

"New Year's Dawn" became "New Year's Dawn, 1947," which speaks to a particular and recollected moment in history that focuses for the reader the various references and attitudes within the poem.

"Inquisitors" was changed to "The Inquisitors," which, of course, both emphasizes and specifies as bearing a sort of ultimate position for the inquisitors.

"Mamouth" was changed to "Original Sin," which addresses not size but the impact and consequences of an act.
3. Robinson Jeffers, Jeffers Collection.
4. Saxe Commins to Robinson Jeffers, April 2, 1953, Jeffers Collection.

REFERENCES

WORKS BY ROBINSON JEFFERS

The Alpine Christ and Other Poems. Previously unpublished poems
from the years 1916-24 compiled with commentary and notes by
William Everson. Aromas, Calif.: Cayucos Books, 1973. Limited
to 250 copies.

"An Artist." Austin, Tex.: J. S. Mayfield, 1928. Privately printed,
limited to 96 copies.

Apology for Bad Dreams. Paris: Harry Ward Ritchie, 1930.
Limited to 30 copies.

Be Angry At the Sun. New York: Random House, 1941.

"The Beaks of Eagles." San Francisco: A. M. Bender by E. Grabhorn Press, 1936. Privately printed.

The Beginning and the End and Other Poems. New York: Random
House, 1963. The last works of Robinson Jeffers.

Californians. New York: Macmillan and Co., 1916. Reprinted with
an introduction by William Everson, Cayucos Books, 1971.

Cawdor and Other Poems. New York: Liveright, 1928. Limited to
375 copies.

Dear Judas and Other Poems. New York: Liveright, 1929. Limited
to 375 copies.

Descent to the Dead. New York: Random House, 1931. Poems
written in Ireland and Great Britain.

The Double Axe and Other Poems. New York: Random House,
1948.

Flagons and Apples. Los Angeles: Grafton Publishing Co. 1912.
Privately printed by Jeffers. Reprinted with an introduction by
William Everson, Cayucos Books, 1970.

Give Your Heart to the Hawks. New York: Random House, 1933.

"Hope Is Not For The Wise." San Mateo, Calif.: Quercus Press,
1937. Limited to 24 copies.

"Hungerfield." San Francisco: Noel Sullivan, 1952. Privately printed. *Hungerfield and Other Poems.* New York: Random House, 1954.

Medea. New York: Random House, 1946. Freely adapted from the *Medea* of Euripides.

Poems. San Francisco: Book Club of California, 1928. With an introduction by B. H. Lehman. Limited to 310 copies.

Poetry, Gongorism and a Thousand Years. Los Angeles: Ward Ritchie Press, 1949. Limited to 200 copies. Reprinted from the *New York Times Magazine,* January 18, 1948.

"Return." San Francisco: Grabhorn Press, 1934. Limited to 250 copies.

Roan Stallion, Tamar and Other Poems. New York: Boni and Liveright, 1925.

Robinson Jeffers' Letters. Random House Collection, Rare Book and Manuscript Library, Columbia University Libraries, Columbia University, New York City.

The Selected Poetry of Robinson Jeffers. New York: Random House, 1938.

Solstice and Other Poems. New York: Random House, 1935. Limited to 320 copies.

"Stars." Pasadena, Calif.: Flame Press, 1930. Limited to 110 copies.

Such Counsels You Gave to Me. New York: Random House, 1937. Limited to 300 copies.

Tamar and Other Poems. New York: P. G. Boyle, 1924.

Themes in My Poems. San Francisco: Book Club of California, 1956. From a 1941 address, "The Poet in Democracy," delivered at the Library of Congress, Washington, D.C.

Thurso's Landing and Other Poems. New York: Liveright, 1932. Limited to 200 copies.

Tor House Papers. Jeffers Collection, Humanities Research Center, The University of Texas, Austin.

"Two Consolations." San Mateo, Calif.: Quercus Press, 1940. With an excerpt from Una Jeffers' English Journal. Limited to 250 copies.

Visits to Ireland. Los Angeles: Ward Ritchie Press, 1954. Travel diaries of Una Jeffers, foreword by Robinson Jeffers. Limited to 300 copies.

The Women at Point Sur. New York: Boni and Liveright, 1927. Limited to 265 copies.

BOOKS BY OTHER AUTHORS

Adamic, Louis. *Robinson Jeffers: A Portrait.* Seattle: University of Washington Book Store, 1929. Chapbook No. 27.

Alberts, Sydney Seymour. *A Bibliography of the Works of Robinson Jeffers.* New York: Random House, 1933. Limited to 487 copies. Reprinted by Cultural History Research, Rye, N.Y., 1966.

Bennett, Melba Berry. *Robinson Jeffers and the Sea.* San Francisco: Gelber, Lilienthal, 1936. Limited to 300 copies.

——. *The Stone Mason of Tor House: The Life and Work of Robinson Jeffers.* Los Angeles: Ward Ritchie Press, 1966.

Bogan, Louise. "Landscape With Jeffers." In *Selected Criticism: Poetry and Prose.* New York: Noonday Press, 1955.

Carpenter, Frederick Ives. *Robinson Jeffers.* New York: Twayne, 1962.

——. "Robinson Jeffers and the Torches of Violence." In *The Twenties: Poetry and Prose,* edited by Richard E. Langford and William E. Taylor, DeLand, Fla.: E. Edwards Press, 1966.

Commager, Henry S. "The Cult of the Irrational." In *The American Mind.* New Haven: Yale University Press, 1950.

De Casseres, Benjamin. *Robinson Jeffers: Tragic Terror.* J. S. Mayfield, 1928. Privately printed, limited to 49 copies. First appeared in *Bookman* 66 (November 1927): 262-66.

Deutsch, Babbette. "A Look at the Worst." In *Poetry in Our Time.* New York: Columbia University Press, 1956.

Everson, William (Brother Antoninus). *Robinson Jeffers: Fragments of an Older Fury.* Berkeley: Oyez Press, 1968.

Gilbert, Rudolph. "Robinson Jeffers. The Philosophic Tragedist." In *Four Living Poets.* Santa Barbara, Calif.: Unicorn Press, 1944.

———. *Shine, Perishing Republic: Robinson Jeffers and the Tragic Sense in Modern Poetry*. Boston: Bruce Humphries, 1936.

Gregory, Horace. "Poet Without Critics: A Note on Robinson Jeffers." In *The Dying Gladiators and Other Essays*. New York: Grove Press, 1961.

Gregory, Horace, and Marya Zaturenska. "Robinson Jeffers and the Birth of Tragedy." In *History of American Poetry 1900-1940*. New York: Harcourt, Brace and Co., 1946.

Monjian, Mercedes C. *Robinson Jeffers: A Study in Inhumanism*. Pittsburgh: University of Pittsburgh Press, 1958.

Powell, Lawrence Clark. *Robinson Jeffers: The Man and His Work*. Los Angeles: Primavera Press, 1934. Decorations by Rockwell Kent. Another edition with decorations by James Hawkins, Pasadena: San Pasquale Press, 1940. These works grew from *An Introduction to Robinson Jeffers,* Powell's dissertation, published in Dijon: Imprimerie Bernigaud and Priva, 1932.

———. "The Making of a Poet." In *Books in My Baggage: Adventures in Reading and Collecting*. Cleveland: World Publishing Co., 1960.

Power, Sister M. J. "Robinson Jeffers." In *Poets At Prayer*. New York: Sheed and Ward, 1938.

Ridgeway, Ann. *The Selected Letters of Robinson Jeffers: 1897-1962*. Baltimore: Johns Hopkins Press, 1968.

Squires, Radcliffe. *The Loyalties of Robinson Jeffers*. Ann Arbor: University of Michigan Press, 1956.

Sterling, George. *Robinson Jeffers: The Man and the Artist*. New York: Boni and Liveright, 1926.

Van Wyck, William. *Robinson Jeffers*. Los Angeles: Ward Ritchie Press, 1938. Limited to 250 copies.

Waggoner, H. H. "Robinson Jeffers: Here is Reality." In *The Heel of Elohim: Science and Values in Modern American Poetry*. Norman, Okla. University of Oklahoma Press, 1950.

Wilder, Amos N. "Nihilism of Mr. Robinson Jeffers." In *The Spiritual Aspects of the New Poetry*. New York: Harper, 1940.

PERIODICALS

Angoff, Charles. "Three Towering Figures: Robert Frost, Robinson Jeffers and William Carlos Williams." *Literary Review.* 6 (1963): 423-29.

Boyers, Robert. "A Sovereign Voice: The Poetry of Robinson Jeffers." *Saturday Review* 1969, 487-507.

Brophy, Robert J. "Tamar, The Cenci, and Incest." *American Literature* 42 (1970): 241-44.

———. "A Textual Note on Robinson Jeffers' *The Beginning and the End.*" *Papers of the Bibliographical Society of America* 60 (1966): 344-48.

Bushby, D. M. "Poets of Our Southern Frontier." *Overland and Out West,* February 1931, pp. 41-42.

Carpenter, Frederick Ives. "Death Comes for Robinson Jeffers." *University Review* 7 (December 1940): 97-104.

———. "Values of Robinson Jeffers." *American Literature* 77 (January 1940): 353-66. A reply by H. M. Jones is in the March 1940 edition, p. 108.

Chatfreld, Hale. "Robinson Jeffers: His Philosophy and His Major Themes." *Laurel Review* 6 (1966), 56-71.

Cunningham, C. C. "The Rhythm of Robinson Jeffers' Poetry as Revealed by Oral Reading." *Quarterly Journal of Speech* 32 (October 1946): 351-57.

Davis, Harold J. "Jeffers Denies Us Twice." Review of *Women at Point Sur. Poetry* 31 (February 1928): 274-79.

Dickey J. "First and Last Things." *Poetry* (February 1964): 320-21.

Fitts, Dudley. "The Hellenism of Robinson Jeffers." *Kenyon Review,* Autumn 1946, pp. 678-83.

Fletcher, James G. "The Dilemma of Robinson Jeffers." *Poetry* 43 (March 1934): 338-42.

Folk, B. N. "Robinson Jeffers Taken to Task." *Catholic World,* July 1954, pp. 270-73.

REFERENCES

Gierasch, Walter. "Robinson Jeffers." *English Journal* 28 (April 1939): 284-95.

Glicksberg, Charles I. "The Poetry of Doom and Despair." *Humanist* 7 (August 1947): 69-76.

Gustafson, Richard. "The Other Side of Robinson Jeffers." *Iowa English Yearbook,* no. 9 (1964): 75-80.

Hackman, Martha. "Whitman, Jeffers, and Freedom." *Prairie Schooner* 20 (Fall 1946): 182-84.

Jerome, J. "Language of Robinson Jeffers." *Writer's Digest,* January 1969, p. 86.

Johnson, W. S. "Savior in the Poetry of Robinson Jeffers." *American Literature,* May 1943, pp. 159-68.

Jorgensen, V. E. "Hearing the Night-Herons: A Lesson on Robinson Jeffers' 'Hurt Hawks.'" *English Journal* 51: 440-42.

Keller, Karl. "California, Yankees, and the Death of God: The Allegory in Jeffers' *Roan Stallion.*" *Texas Studies in Language and Literature* 12: 111-20.

Lilienthal, Theodore M. "The Robinson Jeffers Committee." *Quarterly News Letter* 28: 81.

Littlejohn, David. "Cassandra Grown Tired." *Commonweal* 77: 276-78.

Monroe, Harriet. "Power and Pomp." *Poetry* 28 (June 1926): 160-64.

Morris, Lloyd S. "Robinson Jeffers: The Tragedy of a Modern Mystic." *New Republic* 54 (1928): 386-90.

Nolte, William H. "Robinson Jeffers as a Didactic Poet." *Virginia Quarterly Review* 42: 257-71.

Pinckney, Josephine. "Jeffers and MacLeish." *Virginia Quarterly Review* 8 (July 1932): 443-47.

Powell, Lawrence Clark. "The Double Marriage of Robinson Jeffers." *Southwest Review* 41 (Summer 1956): 278-82.

Rice, Philip Blair. "Jeffers and the Tragic Sense." *Nation,* October 23, 1935, pp. 480-82.

Robinson Jeffers Newsletter. Edited by Melba Berry Bennett (nos. 1-22) and Robert J. Brophy (nos. 23 —). Los Angeles: Robinson Jeffers Committee of Occidental College.

Roddy, J. "View from Granite Tower." *Theatre Arts,* June 1949, pp. 32-36.

Rodman, Seldon. "Knife in the Flowers." *Poetry,* July 1954, pp. 226-31.

———. "Transhuman Magnificence." *Saturday Review of Literature,* July 31, 1948, pp. 13-14. A review of *The Double Axe and Other Poems.*

Rorty, James. "The Ecology of Robinson Jeffers." *Quarterly Newsletter* 32: 32-36.

———. "Symbolic Melodrama." *New Republic,* May 18, 1932, pp. 24-25. Review of *Descent to the Dead* and *Thurso's Landing and Other Poems.*

Schwartz, Delmore. "Sources of Violence" *Poetry* 73 (1949): 30-38.

Short, R. W. *"Tower Beyond Tragedy:* Pain and Death in the Works of Robinson Jeffers." *Southern Review* no. 1 (1941): 132-44.

Smith, Warren Allen. "Authors and Humanism." *Humanist* 11 (October 1951): 193-204.

Sterling, George. "Rhymes and Reactions." *Overland Monthly* 83 (November 1925): 411.

Strickhausen, H. "Recent Criticism." *Poetry,* July 1964, pp. 264-65.

Taylor, Frajam. "The Enigma of Robinson Jeffers: The Hawk and the Stone." *Poetry* 55 (October 1939): 39-46.

Untermeyer, Louis. "Grim and Bitter Dose." *Saturday Review,* January 16, 1954, p. 17.

Van Doren, Mark. "Bits of Earth and Water." *Nation,* January 1929, p. 50. A review of *Cawdor and Other Poems.*

———. "First Glance." *Nation* March 11, 1925, p. 268. A review of *Tamar and Other Poems.*

———. "First Glance." *Nation* July 1927, p. 88. A review of *The Women at Point Sur.*

Waggoner, H. H. "Science and the Poetry of Robinson Jeffers: with the poem 'To Aileen-of-the-Woods.'" *Bibliography of American Literature,* November 1938-January 1939, pp. 495, 275-88.

Watts, H. "Robinson Jeffers and Eating the Serpent." *Sewanee Review,* January 1941, pp. 39-55.

REFERENCES

Wells, Henry W. "The Philosophy of War: The Outlook of Robinson Jeffers." *College English* 6 (November 1944): 81-88.

White, William. "Jeffers and Whitman Briefly." *Serif* 6: 36-39.

Winters, Yvor. "Robinson Jeffers." *Poetry* 35 (February 1930): 279-86.

Zabel, Morton D. "The Problem of Tragedy." *Poetry* 33 (March 1929): 336-40.

ACKNOWLEDGMENTS

Gratitude is expressed to the following for permission to reprint previously published materials, or unpublished materials within their control.

Peter Bennett/Deborah Bennett Busch
For extracts from *The Stone Mason of Tor House,* 1966.

Book Club of California
For extracts from *Themes in My Poems,* copyright © 1956.

The Humanist
For extracts from "Authors and Humanism," October 1951.

Robinson Jeffers Collection (Humanities Research Center
University of Texas, Austin)
For extracts from notes of Robinson Jeffers; letters from him; "Untitled Poem;" extracts from the original "Preface" to *The Double Axe and Other Poems;* assorted letters from Saxe Commins, Bennett Cerf, and Robinson Jeffers; as well as permission to print excised poems from *The Double Axe.*

Robinson Jeffers Literary Properties
For permission to print the excised poems from *The Double Axe:* "Miching Mallecho," "An Ordinary Newscaster," "Fantasy," "Staggering Back Toward Life," "What Odd Expedients," "Pourvou Que Ca Doure," "Curb Science," "War-Guilt," "The Blood Guilt," "Wilson in Hell," as well as permission to reprint from *Be Angry at the Sun and Other Poems,* Random House, 1941.

ACKNOWLEDGMENTS

Johns Hopkins Press
For extract from "Preface" by Ann Ridgway, ed., to *The Selected Letters of Robinson Jeffers,* copyright © Johns Hopkins Press.

Liveright Publishing Company
For lines from the poem "Margrave" in *Thurso's Landing,* 1932.

Lawrence Clark Powell
For extract from *Robinson Jeffers: The Man and His Work,* 1940.

New Republic
For extract from Robert Fitzgerald review of *The Double Axe,* November 1948.

N.Y. Times Book Review
For extract from Dudley Fitts review of *The Double Axe,* August 1948.

Random House
For lines from several poems in *The Double Axe and Other Poems,* 1948; extract from the "Foreword" to *Selected Poetry of Robinson Jeffers,* 1937; and the poem, "Tear Life to Pieces" in *The Beginning and the End,* 1941.

Random House Collection (Rare Book and Manuscript Library, Columbia University Libraries, N.Y.C.)
For letters from Robinson Jeffers and Saxe Commins.

Saturday Review
For extract from Seldon Rodman's review of *The Double Axe,* July 1948.

Time Magazine
For extracts from the two reviews of *The Double Axe,* July and August 1948.

Acknowledgments

University of Michigan Press
For extract from *The Loyalties of Robinson Jeffers,* by Radcliffe Squires, copyright © 1956.

University of Oklahoma Press
For extract from *The Heel of Elohim: Science and Values in Modern American Poetry* by Hyatt Howe Waggoner, copyright © 1950.

University of Pittsburgh Press
For extract from *Robinson Jeffers: A Study in Inhumanism* by Mercedes Cunningham Monjian, copyright © 1958.

The Solution ~~is it a~~   If Attligh...

~~Two~~ Bulls in One Pasture ~~Whom?~~   What Odd Inventions Ex pe...

~~WAYS AND MEANS~~

d, whether by unconscious instinct, or waking, or in a dream, I c

how conscious is God,

es odd means for great purposes. His problem with the human race

its capacities

their ~~extremest~~ limits, ~~yet~~ but limit its power. For how dull were

planet, how ~~shorn~~ mean and splendorless,

all one garden; and man locally omnipotent rested the energies t

need, only

tter need breeds.

The solution of course is war, which both goads

frustrates; and to promote war

at odd inventions!   Hitler

murderous i

scene devices: (the   sel sta

Napoleon,

peoples to leaders   ward hi

The next ch

cerns America and   oture i

between th